Power and Morals

Power and Morals

By MARTIN J. HILLENBRAND

IN LITTERIS
LIBERTAS
1754·1893

Columbia University Press

NEW YORK · 1949

TO MY PARENTS

Foreword

THE WORLD TODAY is scarcely in a happy state. For a while it seemed that the vicious forces of evil and violence represented by fascism and its cult of power-worship would sweep away entirely the associational and institutional framework of what we call Western civilization; and once the Allied Nations had won the victory; and crushed the menace, the problems which remained were gigantic in their scope and fearful in their implication. In the minds of thinking men today there is a great uneasiness deriving from uncertainty about the future and a growing recognition that totalitarianism is not a basic evil but only a symptom—admittedly a horrible symptom—of certain radical defects in our society. Apart from the easy platitudes of popular lecturers and journalists, there has been little of the dewy-eyed and sentimental optimism which characterized the last immediate post-war era; and the war itself was fought by many with a minimum of enthusiasm and a maximum of cynicism.

Such generalizations are not meant to cast discredit upon the many thousands who heroically gave their lives for a cause they believed right and in a struggle which was necessary to preserve from complete extinction certain cherished values and institutions; but the fact remains that our primary animus was a negative one and that our aspirations for the future were and are marred by a sense of gnawing unrest, anticipated frustration, and underlying fear that the evil elemental forces which have been beaten down only by mighty effort are rising again in even more terrible and perhaps more irresistible form. We are aghast at the potentialities of destruction which physical science has given to the modern state at war. Not only can the homes and lives of individuals be blasted away, but the essential material bases of our cultural heritage: the churches, the libraries, the schools, the works of art. Unfortunately, knowledge of modern explosives and weapons is not a prerogative of the man of good will. Under the control of vicious, violent men seeking to dominate whatever the cost, these tremendous new instruments of power can constitute a menace far beyond anything utilized by the conquerors and tyrants of old. The fantastic destructiveness of the atomic bomb underlines a continuing process of discovery and development which leads to a theoretical goal of instantaneous mass extinction.

The winning of the war has not solved our political and social problems; it has merely avoided one perverted attempt at their solution. These problems and their causes largely remain, and basic to them is the problem of power without a solution to which all other attempted remedies must fail. Political scientists often talk completely around the essential problem of power without ever recognizing it. Yet political science must come to grips with the real issues and must offer solutions if the time, effort and intelligence which thousands of students and educators pour into it are to be justified. In this turbulent twentieth century, purely peripheral concentration is a luxury we can ill afford.

There is always an implication of the presumptuous about one who attempts to write of essential solutions; and I should be presumptuous indeed were I to imagine that any book can "solve" the problem of power in the actual order. But an indispensable condition to its solution is a clear idea of just what that problem is. Once we have a clear idea, our discussion will at least be realistic. I hope this book will contribute towards such clarity and realism. It is not concerned with details of

the peace, with specific plans for post-war economic and political rehabilitation and cooperation; for important as these are
on their own level, their ultimate workability depends on the
success with which, in a more fundamental sense, the power that
men have can be directed towards desirable objectives. What
will emerge, I trust, is the outline of a political philosophy in
terms of which power can become the servant of man rather
than the master of his destiny. My debt to the great tradition
of scholastic thought is obvious and acknowledged. Few of
those trained in the intellectual tradition of the "philosophia
perennis" will, after added experience and reflection, refuse to
testify on behalf of its continuing pertinence to the contemporary issues of power.

This is not, however, intended to be a treatise on metaphysics
or epistemology, although it draws on the conclusions of those
studies and attempts to show what a deleterious effect their
neglect has had on political theory. My assumptions should become clear as the discussion continues, and I do not doubt that
these will arouse strong feelings of opposition on the part of
many who are unwilling to admit the implications of their
denial. What those implications are in the sphere of politics I
try to point out, and I can only hope that in the process of intellectual opposition at least some will be led to reexamine
premises which they have long held self-evident or proved.

To inject a further personal note—I have been able to write
the pages which follow only after much discouraging interrup-
tion. They have been partially written, lost and scattered when
Rangoon fell to the Japanese, laboriously reassembled, rewrit-
ten, and finally completed, in the midst of war, civil disturbance
and crisis. Frequent transfer and travel have helped to keep me
separated from notes and library.

Since leaving Columbia University in 1939, I have been stationed as a representative of the United States Government in Switzerland, Burma, India, East Africa, and Germany, with two periods in Washington interspersed. There has been unique opportunity to observe both the use and abuse of power, and the experience of these troubled years has but strengthened the convictions of a more serene academic period. After Pearl Harbor, I witnessed the ravages of Japanese power against a relatively defenseless Burma; and later, while in India, I was in a favorable position to observe the principle of non-violence in practice during the great civil disobedience campaign of 1942, as well as to study at first hand those aspects of Indian thought which are discussed in Chapter VI. More recently, amid the bleak and overwhelming ruins of the formerly great German cities, it has not been difficult to reflect on the precariousness of our civilization faced with the capacity of modern weapons to destroy in a night what it has taken over a thousand years to build, on the feebleness of inhibition, once men are power-mad like the Nazis, against risking all for the attainment of perverse objectives.

During the somewhat labored completion of this volume I have had the patient encouragement of Professors Lindsay Rogers and Schuyler Wallace of Columbia University for which I can only express my gratitude. At a later stage the constructive criticism of Professors Robert M. MacIver, John M. Clark, and Herbert W. Schneider, all of Columbia University, has likewise proved most helpful. It should be noted, however, that the views expressed herein, for which I accept full responsibility, do not necessarily coincide with theirs.

Thanks are also due to the following publishing houses for their kind permission to quote short passages from books and periodicals published by them: The Cambridge University Press, Otto von Gierke, *Natural Law and the Theory of Society*

(1934); The Carnegie Endowment for International Peace, James Brown Scott, *The Spanish Conception of International Law and of Sanctions* (1934); Victor Gollancz, Ltd., Leonard Woolf, *Barbarians at the Gate* (1939); Harper & Brothers, Dorothy Fosdick, *What Is Liberty?* (1939), and Aldous Huxley, *Ends and Means* (1937); The Harvard University Press, Benjamin F. Wright, Jr., *American Interpretations of Natural Law* (1931); B. Herder Book Co., Etienne Gilson, *Moral Values and the Moral Life* (1931); The Modern Schoolman, Vol. XIII (1936), Timothy Brosnahan, *"Ethics: a Science";* The Oxford University Press, Ernest Barker, *Political Thought in England from Herbert Spencer to the Present Day* (1924), J. L. Brierly, *The Outlook for International Law* (1944), and A. J. Carlyle, *Political Liberty* (1941).

MARTIN J. HILLENBRAND

Bremen, Germany
July, 1948

Contents

Contents

PART I

The Problem of Power

I

Power and the Role of Theory

POWER IS A FACT, and so is the desire of men for it. As humans
are constituted, it is a basic phenomenon of political and social
life, either as a motive for conduct for those who desire it, or,
when possessed, as something used to achieve desired ends. This
is not to say it is the only motive which moves men to action, or
even, as Bertrand Russell asserts, the chief desire of men.[1] Certainly many men want other things more. But certainly too, it is
an important desire of men, and in those whom it dominates can
be ruthless and overwhelming, sweeping aside or crushing without mercy all obstacles to its attainment. As Lord Russell correctly points out,[2] the desire for power is closely allied to the
desire for glory, and since usually the easiest way to obtain glory
is to obtain power, the two motives prompt, in the main, the
same actions, and may often for most practical purposes be
considered as one.

Once achieved, power is extremely likely to be abused; in
fact, the very process of getting it may have been such as to
make its abuse almost certain. Thus when violence is used to
achieve and maintain power, a tradition and habit of violence
are gradually formed so that it becomes exceedingly difficult
for those in power to forbear from violence whenever a desired

[1] *Power, a New Social Analysis,* London, 1938, p. 9.
[2] *Ibid.*

end can be accomplished by its use.[3] The mere possession of great power, with its attendant glory and access to luxury, can corrupt, though not always with the inevitability implied by Lord Acton's famous dictum. Powerful men often become ever more intolerant of criticism and opposition, more unfeeling to subordinates, and more reluctant to recognize any limits to their power.

There are of course many different kinds of power. If we define the term in its broadest sense as the ability to produce intended effects or effects which may possibly be intended,[4] we can find scarcely any sphere of human activity where it does not exist to a greater or lesser degree. Even the poor Indian peasant, bound to a life of grinding poverty and backbreaking toil, has power—over his water buffalo, his wife, his son. The ability to produce intended effects is inherent in any system of relationship between man and man, or between man and his environment.

But power in this broad sense is obviously not what men fear. They fear power which can affect adversely their lives, the lives of those whom they love, or more generally, the institutions, associations, and allegiances to which they are devoted. They fear economic power which can doom them to a life of unrewarded toil and insecurity, or social power which can relegate them to a position of inferiority or ostracize them completely from a community, or make impossible a desired mode of life. But primarily, because to a large extent it is the ultimate sanction of all other power that really coerces men against their will,

[3] See Aldous Huxley, *Ends and Means,* London and New York, 1937, pp. 25 ff., for an illuminating discussion of this phenomenon. See also below, pp. 111 ff.

[4] Bertrand Russell has defined power as "the production of intended effects" (*op. cit.,* p. 35), but since power obviously may exist but not be used, it is desirable to define it in terms of potentiality rather than activity.

they fear antagonistic physical power, the power of force. Force implies the use of violence, potential or actual, to coerce or to destroy those who will not be coerced.

Up to the present, the highest expression of physical power is that found in the state as exerted through its various agencies of force—the police, the army, and the navy. That is, however, not to identify the state with force, or to define the state purely as a power-institution. But the power of force is certainly its ultimate concrete sanction, just as the possession of this power, at least to some degree, is a necessary characteristic.

Much of the contemporary uneasiness about the future rises out of a recognition in some, and in most perhaps only a vague awareness, that modern civilization does not contain within itself the means through which this power of force may be controlled. They sense that it is not merely a matter of arriving at new institutional formulae, of building a United Nations Organization, or of modifying existing dictatorships and police states. These measures may be indispensable to peace, may even insure it for a time, but in themselves seem inadequate without some additional basis of control over the possessors of power which will militate against its perversion to evil ends, even though vested in originally good institutions.

There are two fundamental ways by which the power of force may be controlled; (1) by the threat of, or the actual use of, superior power of force, or (2) by the pressure of criteria of conduct on the possessors of power. While it is true that economic power may sometimes, through its control over production, defy the power of force in the same sense that, in a totalitarian state, a skilled scientist whose research is valuable to arms production may with impunity fail to conform to certain requirements imposed on other men—yet, in the last analysis, the greatest power of force can always be supreme on the material plane, for it can always destroy by violence that which has less power of force. No matter how brave and resolute the opposition, how noble its motives and principles, violence—if there is enough of it—can crush such opposition. If it is not crushed, then there simply is not enough power of force available for the purpose.[5]

In the last analysis any institutional control over the power of force must dispose of superior power of force if it is to maintain itself against all challenge. Economic sanctions may deter, then again they may not. But the ability of a greater power of force to control a lesser, while a fact, is in itself utterly inadequate; for there always remains the further problem of controlling the greater power, whether it be a national state, an alliance of states, a regional federation, or a world union. Even in the latter still very theoretical case, the abuse of power is certainly possible. It cannot be emphasized enough that institutions as such never exercise power; it is always the men in charge of institutions, whether national or international, who have power. This is true even in a democracy, although the democratic process insures greater diffusion of power and control of policy from below. It does not guarantee, of course, that the very process of democracy cannot be used by the enemies of democracy, as in the Weimar Republic, to seize power and establish tyranny. New dictators may rise, perhaps in a new context broader than the national state, misusing the power which new institutions give them; although in our time it seems likely that the chief disturbers of peace will continue to be rulers of national states or allied combinations of them.

The essential solution, then, to the problem of physical power

[5] See below, Chap. VI *passim*, for a discussion of the power of non-violence against violence.

cannot be found on the plane of physical power. In so far as it is possible to "solve" any basic social problem in this world of weak, inconsistent, passionate, and sometimes evil men, it can only be found in the establishment and general recognition of criteria for the use of power and of obligation to observe those criteria. Such criteria must obviously be those which men of good will generally agree are desirable and necessary; for power is seldom used entirely without discrimination—even the worst tyrant has certain objectives, be they only the increase of his own power and possessions.

But when we talk of "criteria," of "men of good will," we make certain basic assumptions about the nature of human conduct, which raise the entire question of how much, if at all, theory, standards, criteria can influence and regulate the action of men in their private lives and as the possessors of power.

THEORY AND PRACTICE

Many have denied an active formative role to ideas and to theory in the molding of human conduct and institutions, among them men like Karl Marx whose theories have been of major importance in the making of the twentieth century world. The *theory* that conditions create ideas, without any *vice versa*, has been a common modern presupposition even in the midst of the great ideological struggles of the past decade; and not all of those who hold this view are necessarily dialectical materialists in the strict Marxist sense. Professor E. M. Sait, for example, in his popular textbook rides full tilt into those so foolish as to suppose that the ideals of men can shape their political conduct.[6] In the field of pure literature, the naturalist school of Zola and the early Huysmans still influences many writers in their approach

[6] See his *Political Institutions*, New York, 1938, pp. 3 ff.

to social as well as individual conduct, with its extreme crudities perhaps replaced by the refinements of Freudian or behavioristic psychology.

Such a deterministic position is at least understandable. Why one should write a book about it which cannot possibly, as a medium of ideas, influence anyone's conduct is less easily understood; determinism is scarcely consistent with the zeal for reform that so frequently accompanies it. Certainly the reformer must have not only an idea beforehand as to what kind of conditions he prefers, but also some implicit belief that he can do something positive to change existing conditions in the direction of his ideal.

Leonard Woolf has stated this contradiction between principle and practice with brilliant sarcasm:

It is fashionable today to believe that ideas have little or no effect upon the social history of human beings, that history is determined only by violence and by economics. This is one of the grossest and strangest delusions that have entered the muddled brain of that distracted political animal, man, and one of the strangest things about it is that those who are among the most fervent propagators of the delusion are also those who spend an immense amount of time and energy in trying to get political ideas into the heads of the masses in order that the masses may do what the propagators want them to do.[7]

To maintain that ideas do not affect human acts and institutions is to "adopt a view of individual and social psychology which is contradicted, not only by the facts of history, but by the behaviour and assumptions of all statesmen, politicians, and political thinkers, no matter what may be their nationality, class, party or ideology." [8]

An objective examination of the human past scarcely seems to verify any strictly deterministic interpretation of history, and

[7] *Barbarians at the Gate*, London, 1939, p. 108.
[8] *Ibid.*, p. 58.

modern historians are more and more veering away from the simplicist and mechanistic explanations of a Taine or Buckle.[9] Marxists will still call any non-deterministic theory of history "idealism," but this usage is misleading in the present context. The terms "realism" and "idealism" have acquired all sorts of conflicting meanings, and Marx has contributed as much as anyone to the confusion with his false dichotomy between "idealism" and "materialism." A young Marxist once blithely informed the writer that St. Thomas Aquinas was a prime example of an idealist; this, of course, is absurd in the light of traditional philosophic terminology, especially when one remembers that the University of Paris nearly managed to get the great scholastic condemned for what it considered his excessive realism.

We cannot deny the influence of environment upon ideas or theory,[10] since we obviously cannot think correctly about anything unless we know something about it; and much of what we know derives from our physical environment. But the institutions and the conduct of men do involve ideas, vague or deeply buried in the accumulation of custom and habit as some of these may be; and other ideas can affect changes in institu-

[9] The conversion of Dr. Charles A. Beard a decade ago to the philosophy of *historismus* was a significant straw in the wind; and though there is a great deal of muddled thinking mixed up with the modern reaction to deterministic history, the trend is a healthy one. In the other social sciences a book like Professor Karl Mannheim's *Ideology and Utopia*, New York, 1936, has exerted considerable influence with its extreme relativism and anti-causationalism. Few members of these new schools have, of course, declared themselves out-and-out voluntarists, for the hold of the old shibboleths is still strong. See Charles A. Beard, *The Discussion of Human Affairs*, New York, 1936, especially Chap. XI; also his article, "History and Social Science," *Saturday Review of Literature*, XII (1935), 9; and Charles A. Beard and Alfred Vagts, "Currents of Thought in Historiography," *American Historical Review*, XLII (1937), 460.

[10] In this discussion the term "idea" is used in the popular sense, which is broader than mere "concept" or result of the abstractive power of the active intellect, to which the strict Aristotelian or scholastic might prefer to limit it.

tions and individual conduct. This does not mean, of course, that clear-cut ideas are chronologically prior to all institutions or action, for social groupings and arrangements often grow out of basic human needs, and individual conduct may be the result of a complex of motives and drives. But in the going world of today, ideas do underlie new institutional forms, new types of conduct, just as they help maintain the old ones even if only as *ex post facto* rationalizations. There is a constant interplay between universals and their actualizations.[11]

One need not agree with this analysis, but can maintain instead that ideas have no causal effect on institutions or conduct. In that case one also ought to stop having ideas. They are such a waste of time.

But men will not stop having ideas. Professed determinists will continue to propose and fight for programs which, according to their principles, can have no possible effect on the conduct of men and their affairs. Such a basic illogicality, however, has in the long run had disastrous results, and is, as we shall see, not least among those failures of theory which have been such potent factors in bringing the affairs of men to their present state of uncertainty, and in permitting brute power to run amuck free from inhibition.

Even the strictest determinist cannot deny that there are only two broad possible types of control over the power of force: the external control of superior power, actually or potentially applied, and the internal control of self-restraint in the use of power based on some criterion or theory of conduct. Superior power may, of course, be used in accordance with such criterion in order to control abuse by lesser power. But if the role of the-

---

[11] For a profound analysis of the relationship of metaphysical form to its actualization, see E. I. Watkin, *A Philosophy of Form*, London, 1935, especially Chap. I.

ory is pure illusion, then there can be no check to superior power other than that imposed upon it by fortuitous circumstance and predetermined causation. The problem of power becomes entirely a matter of physics, chemistry, and uncontrollable human drives, and any attempt at an analysis of power can have no more relation to its control then a treatise on the properties of earthquakes or typhoons. That, of course, is sheer nonsense.

A prerequisite to any intelligent discussion of the problem of power is the concession of some role to theory—theory which establishes standards for the use of power. Such theory must necessarily involve a certain obligation to observe the standards established. Otherwise it serves chiefly to assist those who recognize the lack of obligation in making dupes of the hapless many. As our analysis continues, we shall see that the only kind of theory which does provide both criteria and obligation in the political sphere—the primary sphere of physical power—is one based on a valid system of ethics the observance of which is a matter of moral obligation. Such a politico-ethical theory cannot stand in a vacuum. To invite intellectual assent, to possess coherence, it must be an integral part of a general philosophy; and its validity must ultimately depend on the validity of that philosophy. The metaphysical basis of politics is not only a reality but a necessity, and the failure of modern political thinkers is not merely a failure to grasp the essential problem of power but a failure to realize the implications of their own basic philosophies, which logically can be used to justify many of those abuses of power which so plague our modern world and which they are first to decry.

It is true, of course, despite the necessary role which theory must play in human affairs, that general acceptance *in theory* of an ethical code does not guarantee it will not be violated. A wide gap often separates principle and actual practice. Human nature being what it is, there will always be those who succumb to the lure of power and glory and misuse such power as they possess. On the other hand, lacking ethical criteria, more individuals will tend to misuse power; in fact, without such criteria the very concept of misuse loses meaning. The use of power to achieve desired ends becomes a legitimate means under all circumstances, and the only restraint need be conflicting power. Between those who would misuse power whether or not they profess an ethical code, and those who for temperamental or other reasons would never flagrantly abuse power even if they completely lack an ethical code, come the great majority of men who will ordinarily be restrained by such a code, but who, lacking one, will attempt to get away with whatever they can. It is this group which may fall either into the category of brawling storm-troopers, strutting SS guards and tyrannical Gauleiters, or into the category of decent law-abiding citizens leading normal, useful lives.

A certain dualism of conduct often found in statesmen likewise works against the pure effectiveness of ethical theory. A leader of men may be an exceedingly moral person in his private life, yet as a maker of policy entirely amoral in terms of the same criteria. This pigeon-hole mentality which, for example, permitted the famous Iron Chancellor to practice power politics to the utmost at the Foreign Office and at the same time be a pious Lutheran husband in his home, is all too common, but certainly not because of inexorable necessity. Contrast such a picture with that of the statesman of integrity who sincerely guides his official conduct by high principle. No matter how prone men are to ignore or water down inconvenient precepts, there are, for those who accept it, certain broad criteria of conduct in the traditional Western moral code which cannot be rationalized away or bent to suit the need. How otherwise explain the evident difference between a Napoleon and a Jefferson, a Ribbentrop and a Cordell Hull?

Those who plead the cause of ethical theory must, however, caution themselves against a common overemphasis. Theory is not all, and by itself is not likely to be enough. It is an indispensable condition to the good society, not the only condition. The importance of economic and social factors in the rise to power of Hitler and Mussolini, and the growth of their mass following, should not be minimized. But it remains true that just as Caesarism brought loss of liberty to Rome at a time of general moral collapse, so the ruthless abuse of power characteristic of twentieth century dictatorships has come in an era of large-scale abandonment of ethical standards. The discussion in the chapters which follow should show, among other things, that these concurrent developments have been far from purely coincidental.

II

The Totalitarian Challenge

IN AN AGE of revolutionary change, distintegrating cultures and
general turmoil, the modern totalitarian state has posed the basic
problem of political theory—the control of power—in its most
pressing form. The New Leviathan involves modes of conduct
completely antithetical to those which men of good will have
held necessary for decent human existence and welfare. Not
only did the Nazi leaders, for example, repudiate in theory most
of the values which had been integrated into Western culture,
but they attempted through the use of power to destroy those
values and to impose their own primitive and savage outlook.
They flaunted a code of unrestrained lying and duplicity, unmitigated force and violence, threatening, almost with success,
to sweep away centuries of political and social progress in an
orgy of blood and cruelty.[1]

For thinking men the victory of our arms, though neces-

[1] Apart from those who contributed to the plethora of wartime books
about Germany, books which may broadly be classified as either pro or
anti-Vansittart in tendency, many pre-war writers emphasized the an-
tithesis between the Nazi and traditional Western values. Thus while Professor Melvin Rader's *No Compromise, the Conflict between Two
Worlds*, London, 1939, is somewhat shrill, his indictment rings substantially true. The same may be said for Hamilton Fish Armstrong's *We or
They*, New York, 1937; Aurel Kolnai's *War against the West*, New York,
1938, or Hermann Raushning's *The Revolution of Nihilism*, New York,
1939. A more subtle analysis may be found in Peter Drucker's *The End of
Economic Man*, New York, 1939; or in Christopher Dawson's *Religion
and the Modern State*, London, 1935.

sary, has obviously provided small assurance in itself that from now on the world will be free from the abuse of power. Modern amoral totalitarianism is symptomatic of certain basic deficiencies in our society and culture; and the abuse of power which it manifests is ever likely as long as the causal factors from which it originally springs continue to exist. Into the making of this modern totalitarianism have gone three main streams of causation: the bad will of men, the bad theories upon which men have acted, and a complexus of social, economic, and institutional factors—all of which have interacted upon each other. It is true, therefore, that we cannot accurately discuss the fascist or communist state purely in theoretical terms, and that is the weakness of all purely negative diatribes against the totalitarian ideology. The great merit in the approach of writers like Christopher Dawson and Ross Hoffman is that they picture totalitarianism as an attempted adjustment of state function—though a perverted one —to the ever-increasing formlessness, distintegration and, withal, complexity of modern life, a problem which liberal political and social theory has failed utterly to meet.[2]

On the other hand, it is important to recognize for example that, within their context of a crumbling German social and economic order, the Nazis represented not only a triumph of evil and maliciousness, but also of bad theory. And it is likewise important to recognize that this bad theory did not necessarily derive solely from the Nazi philosophy as such but owed some obligation as well to certain other currents of Western thought. If modern political theory has reached an impasse on the prob-

---

[2] See Dawson's *Religion and the Modern State*, also his *Beyond Politics*, London, 1939, and *The Judgment of the Nations*, New York, 1942; and Professor Hoffman's *The Will to Freedom*, New York, 1935, and *Tradition and Progress*, Milwaukee, 1938. Only a superficial reader will confuse their analysis with that of a cynical pro-fascist writer like Lawrence Dennis.

lem of power, it is the inevitable result of compartmentalized liberal thinking by which a man could be both philosophic nihilist and democratic progressive without noting any contradiction. This mental "spherism" which permitted a man to hold two basically incompatible positions ran all through the last century; the attacks of scientific materialism forced certain sensitive religious writers like William Mallock to go so far as to actually postulate two levels of truth, the religious and the empirical, which could apparently be contradictory and yet both be true—almost a return to medieval Averroism.

The curse of unrealized implications hung over the nineteenth century; today, in the twentieth century, implications are not only realized, but accepted and acted upon. By undermining the ethical basis of politics, though still advocating moral objectives in political practice, liberal writers like Bentham, Mill, and Morley helped to open the way to a non-ethical politics in both theory and practice among more logical thinkers on the Continent. A steady diet of nominalism, positivism, associationism, epiphenomenalism, extreme natural selection, and all the rest, could only lead either to acute mental indigestion or to an unmitigated *Machtpolitik*. Though they probably would have been aghast at the thought, the great English liberals are in certain implications much closer to Machiavelli, Nietzsche, Houston Chamberlain, and Hitler than many of the conservative writers whom they attacked as opposed to the interests of the people.

Opinions on the real nature of liberalism may range from the antagonistic economic interpretation of Marxist Harold Laski to its defense by John Dewey as an essentially humanitarian movement. Actually it was a little of everything: more a climate of opinion and emotion rather than a fixed credo—drawing on various sources and differing from country to country in point of emphasis—which affected some with zeal for social reform, others with zeal for maximum economic productivity, others with zeal for self-government and the elimination of political privilege, others with kindly if vague sentiments towards beasts and men, and still others merely with boundless optimism and belief in progress. But regardless of what liberalism itself stood for, many of its proponents did espouse philosophic doctrines basically incompatible with moral values and the dignity of the individual. While a noted Catholic priest like Lacordaire could claim the designation of liberal, the leading representatives of nineteenth century liberalism were dominantly utilitarian, positivist, and secularist in their thought.[3]

Truly enough, "all those ideals which we regard as typically Western—the supremacy of law, the recognition of the moral rights of the individual and the duty of society towards the poor and the oppressed," [4] found their most eloquent defenders among the liberals. The reference here is, of course, to what may be called humanitarian liberalism rather than to the strict economic liberalism of the Manchester School. Prior to the Popular Front program of 1936, communists used to lump all liberals together in one species, condemning them *en masse* and forgetting that most of the really vital social as well as political reform movements of the last century were liberal in inspiration.[5] A better-balanced viewpoint will admit the great debt of the Western world to liberalism while recognizing the need for a more structurally consistent basis for values and action in our time.

Amid the relative peace and prosperity of the last century, it seemed as if at least the northwestern European world was mov-

[3] See below, pp. 24 ff.
[4] Christopher Dawson, *Religion and the Modern State*, London, 1935, p. 140.
[5] For a sympathetic evaluation of the liberal contribution see Christopher Dawson's *The Judgment of the Nations*, Chap. IV. See also William Aylott Orton, *The Liberal Tradition*, New York, 1945.

ing inexorably onward and upward, though the poor slum child festering in a squalid Glasgow or London tenement might not have appreciated the fact. The new evolutionary dogmas provided apparent scientific confirmation of the theory of inevitable progress; and with reform bill after reform bill being adopted by the governments of Western countries, it was only natural that political and social optimism should dominate the era and be the prevailing mood among men of good will.[6]

Our generation has finished with all that. Optimism based on belief in inevitable progress received its mortal wound in 1914, though the stimulant of economic boom revived it and kept it speciously alive during the twenties. The process has played itself out; and no matter how much men tell themselves that everything is going to be all right, when they are wholly honest with themselves, they no longer face the future with real confidence and assurance but rather with uncertainty, fear, and bewilderment. It is true that the recent war, by providing objectives requiring immediate concentration and effort, temporarily gave to many a new purpose and to some even a new enthusiasm, which for the time being overshadowed what was becoming apparent in the pre-war era—the ideological bankruptcy of liberal humanitarianism. A few years ago nothing was more pathetic than the floundering of the liberal men of good will, the "good pagans," who saw their world crumbling all about them, their ideals trampled on, sheer power running wild, and who were beginning to feel that basically they did not know what to do about it. As the excitement and distorted perspectives of the recent war clear away, many again find themselves in the same

[6] For an illuminating discussion of the "theory of progress" and of the latter-day reaction to it by modern historians, anthropologists, and philosophers, see Christopher Dawson's *Progress and Religion*, London, 1940, especially Chaps. I–III.

position, lacking not only a basic program for the preservation of their ideals but even a valid reason for such a program.

The humanitarian liberal has been living on the heritage of the ethical past. Espousing traditional Western political and social ideals, he proceeded to deny away every reason for accepting them by rejecting the philosophy from which they derived. Such an unreal structure of moral imperatives was doomed to collapse; for it is impossible to preserve the positive values in a political or social theory while repudiating their metaphysical and epistemological basis. In a general sense "the ethical idealism which was characteristic of nineteenth century culture is passing away with the culture that gave it birth," [7] but the logical and amoral totalitarians have not waited for the working out of historic processes. The Nazi leaders, for example, completely rejected the traditional ethics; and, paradoxically enough, their very logicality led them to illogicality. Having been nurtured on nominalism, determinism, and materialism, they did not hesitate to go the whole hog by denying the very idea of a rational approach to reality, of a rational theory of knowledge. In a perverse sense, Nazi anti-intellectualism, the cult of blood and feeling, was intellectualism to the utmost. The ideals of democracy, individual rights, the rule of law become ridiculous if men are but lumps of mud, their highest aspirations but fluctuations of matter. Only force remains to settle all issues; nothing is left but "the naked reality of power and no higher principle of the moral order on which to base it." [8]

Once superior power of force had crushed the Nazis and the Fascists, we seemingly had an opportunity to build a world order which would give to nations and individuals a greater measure of freedom from oppression and want than they have

[7] Christopher Dawson, *Religion and the Modern State*, London, 1935, p. 127.   [8] *Ibid.*, p. 138.

hitherto enjoyed. But all our new and revived institutions of cooperation and control were doomed to be in vain unless they rested on a firm foundation of ethical theory commonly accepted and acted upon by the leaders of men as well as their followers. Without ethical criteria for its use, the possessors of power will continue to abuse power.

The unfortunate fact is, however, that no such firm ethical foundation for politics exists today which commands the general assent of men. The victory of the United Nations could not in itself make modern thought less ethically bankrupt. It is true that a large body of individuals, in all activities of life—though a minority at most, and certainly a relatively smaller proportion in liberal intellectual circles—still professes adherence to the traditional Christian faith and moral code, even if itself affected to a greater or lesser degree by the breakdown of standards around it. It is likewise true that, in England and the United States, our publicists, our educators, our political scientists, our leaders, have still to face the full implications of what many of them believe about the nature of man and the universe, and in the meanwhile are content, in their political and social ideals, to continue living on borrowed ethical capital. But such a situation is unsatisfactory and highly unstable. It gives little assurance that the trend towards political amorality and abuse of power so characteristic of our time will not continue. The ideological conditions are ripe for power politics, and there is no lack of men filled with lust for power and willing to be ruthless in its achievement, men freed from all moral inhibition by their awareness of at least the broad implications of modern thought.

As the atomic era dawns, genial skepticism or placid optimism, "Couéism" in the political and social sphere, are as *passé* as the weapons of the Franco-Prussian War. If humanitarianism, scientific positivism, and liberal millenniarism have all crumbled away in this dynamic, power-surging world—then the man of good will must find stronger moorings, or he and the institutions he has fought for are doomed to perish.

III

The Failure of Modern Theory

WE HAVE INDICATED that political thought today is to a great extent ethically bankrupt and hence unable to cope with its basic problem—the control of power—the essential solution to which must lie in the inducement of restraint in the possessors of power so that they will use it only in accordance with certain criteria. These criteria may be broadly described as those which men of good will generally agree upon as desirable, and would include, for example, the axiom that power is a trust and not an inherent right. Some obvious corollaries would be that power should be used for the greatest common good, that it should not be used for personal aggrandizement at the expense of the many, that the use of force is only justifiable as a last resort in order to effect a necessary and proportionate good, and that certain uses of force are never legitimate, no matter what the end in view, because of their debasing effect on the user or because of their utter cruelty and essential inhumanity.

If, as we have claimed, the curse of unrealized implications hangs over and vitiates most modern political thinking, it is important to clarify just what those implications are and why they are necessary implications. There is little point, of course, in mere logomachy. Definitions of political science are numerous, and to many it means nothing more than the result of observation and correlation of facts about the state. But few political scientists are willing to stop there and disclaim all interest in the formulation of ends and the evaluation of events in terms of extra-political criteria. They continually make the value-judgments involved in any definite position on the purpose of government, the legitimate use of power, or the desirability of democracy, civil rights, and personal liberty. Thus willy-nilly they indulge in that political theorizing often so patronizingly dismissed by some of the more "hardheaded" members of the fraternity.

Now political value-judgments cannot be concocted in a vacuum with no relation to anything but political phenomena. Any such value-judgments necessarily imply certain assumptions outside the sphere of politics proper. These may involve the validity of human knowledge, the reality of free will, the function of institutions, or the purpose of existence itself; and these all-important assumptions should logically determine the entire animus and direction of any political theory based thereon. In other words, political theory cannot be divorced from general philosophy, of which it forms an integral part; and the general philosophy of the consistent political theorist must be the foundation, acknowledged or implied, of his political theory. As long as the political scientist insists on making value-judgments, he cannot afford to ignore that discipline from which his presuppositions derive, even though it may mean occasional journeying in what is often conceived to be the cloudland of metaphysics.

Most contemporary political thinkers unfortunately keep going round in circles, making one value-judgment after another but unable to justify any of them as part of a coherent general philosophy. The result is inability to overcome by any logically satisfying argument the position of the modern Machiavellian, who is only too willing to carry out the implications of the basic philosophy of life which he may well share in common with inconsistent liberals opposing his political views. Whether a person merely fails to see that value-judgments without a firm and rational foundation cannot stand, or directly espouses a philosophy which is essentially incompatible with such value-judgments as he may make in the political sphere, he can make no positive contribution to a solution of the moral problem of power.

The ethical control of power involves both the establishment of standards of conduct and of obligation to observe those standards. Yet so many modern men of good will, who can provide the general standards from their heritage of ethical capital, are able to offer no compelling reason either for selecting those particular standards or for obligation to observe them. To be effective, the reason for such standards must be clear and the obligation towards them must be strong enough to influence the individual so that he feels morally constrained to choose a compatible mode of conduct.

In the past century and a half, there have been three common and essentially secular lines of approach to the problem of power: the positivist-utilitarian-pragmatist, the contractualist, and the legalist. Of these, the first and the third have emphasized largely the aspect of criteria or standards, and the second the aspect of obligation. None has proved adequate by itself or in synthesis with the others, but each deserves scrutiny as indicative of the tangents on which modern theory has wandered off.

POSITIVISTS, UTILITARIANS, PRAGMATISTS: BIRDS OF A FEATHER

Positivists, utilitarians, and pragmatists may appropriately be considered together since, allowing for differences of emphasis, they generally find their standard of conduct in what is scientifically observable, in what proves useful, in what works. Truly enough, the proponents of positivism and pragmatism have stressed method more than goal; while the utilitarians, particularly those of the Bentham-Mill school, have considered it necessary to elaborate arguments to prove their goal a logical one. But common to all three is a violent abhorrence of metaphysics and of any ethical system based on what they conceive to be metaphysics. (Actually, of course, no philosophy, political or otherwise, can escape being metaphysical, for even the very denial of metaphysics raises basic metaphysical issues.) The modern pragmatist frequently claims to be a positivist, and vice versa; and the utilitarian generally prides himself on his positivistic method. The basic unity of the three positions shows itself in the logical progression which is possible from one to another in any direction. They hang together and fall together.

There is no denying that something can be said for all three, or that, at certain times and under certain circumstances, a great deal can be said for them—though many say it for the wrong reasons. As limited methodology, positivism and pragmatism are certainly good as far as they go. Only fools will dispute that the experimental method is desirable in regard to those objects which permit its use, but it is a dangerous *non sequitur* to conclude immediately that no other objects exist. That is exalting mere method to the level of criterion of being, or shrinking reality to fit it into a test tube.

Any elementary history of philosophy will note that Auguste Comte is the father of positivism; and this statement seems true enough so far as inventing the term and building a whole system around the "positivistic method" are concerned. In his mammoth *Cours de philosophie positive*, with its famous law of the

three stages of knowledge,[1] he proceeded to discard metaphysical speculation and all concomitants like absolutes, essences, and final and efficient causes.[2] In the third or positive
stage of human knowledge, man has supposedly thrown all such
intellectual claptrap out the window, realizing that his knowledge extends only to facts and those relations of facts which
he calls laws. "Facts," of course, are things observable by the
senses.

Such was the rather flimsy basis of positivism as a philosophy,
and it is certainly significant that Comte himself soon wandered far from the little circle of legitimate knowledge he had
drawn. Nor did French thinkers take kindly to the new dogma,
excepting the lexicographer Littré who, like Comte, moved
farther and farther from pure positivism as he grew older.
Instead it drifted across the Channel, there to nourish the prevailing craze for empiricism and to provide a new systematiza-
tion. Oxford dons like Congrave, Beesly, Bridges, and Harrison
became enthusiastic converts; and even John Stuart Mill accepted Comte as methodological teacher.[3] In so far as positivism
meant greater use of the experimental method in the social
sciences, it was all to the good; but unfortunately Mill and his
followers did not stop there. Failing to grasp the essential limitation of the positivist approach, they did not realize that a

[1] The law itself had already found germinal statement in Turgot. See his
*Recherches sur les causes des progrès et de la décadence des sciences et
des arts; ou, Réflexion sur l'histoire des progrès de l'esprit*, in *Oeuvres*
(5 vols., Paris, 1913), Vol. I, pp. 116–142. See also Alfred Fouillée, *Histoire
de la philosophie*, 3d ed., Paris, 1897, p. 426.
[2] The *Cours* was published in 1839–1942, and a translation by Harriet
Martineau into English in 1853. See also E. Caird, *The Social Philosophy
and Religion of Comte*, 3d ed., Paris, 1913.
[3] See his *Comte and Positivism*, London, 1865; also his discussion of method
in the social sciences in Book Six of the *Logic*, London, 1843. The great
influence of Comte on Mill is not always appreciated by students of nineteenth century English thought.

mere methodology, no matter from where imported, could not straighten out the vicious ethical circle around which pure utilitarianism must revolve.

It is a tedious task, of no particular value here, to trace the complicated interaction of positivism and utilitarianism in the political thought of the last one hundred years—just as these two in turn influenced and were influenced by pragmatism. Though later in time, at least in acquiring a name, pragmatism like positivism amounted to little more than a theory of knowledge masquerading some very dubious value-judgments. Truly enough, it found in William James a subtle statement which went far beyond the capacity of most of his followers, who emphasized the criteria of usefulness or workability and more or less overlooked the epistemological basis provided by his "continuum psychology." [4] But even assuming with James that experience is a continuous whole out of which the mind consciously selects elements *useful* according to its own interests and purposes, that the conscious self not only selects from this whole, and selects purposively, but attributes reality to what it selects—we are still going around in a circle as far as arriving at any scale of values is concerned.

"Useful" is one of those lulling words which seems to say a lot more than it actually does. Useful for what? Things are not useful or workable per se but only in relation to some objective. To some that objective may be purely and unmitigatedly a selfish one—a harsh creed separated only by the centuries from Hobbes' "egoistic utilitarianism." But the clas-

[4] The real logical successor to James is Hans Vaihinger with his philosophy of "as if." See below, p. 36.

The principal works of James expounding his pragmatic philosophy are: *Principles of Psychology*, Boston, 1890; *The Will to Believe*, Boston, 1897; *Pragmatism*, Boston, 1907; *A Pluralistic Universe*, Boston, 1909; *The Meaning of Truth*, Boston, 1909; *Some Problems of Philosophy*, Boston 1911; *Essays in Radical Empiricism*, Boston, 1912.

sical utilitarian doctrine, formulated by Jeremy Bentham [5] and James Mill,[6] and furbished by John Stuart Mill,[7] is much less direct. Utility remains the great touchstone, but it is defined to mean simply the power of an action to produce happiness. Apparently then, the more happiness the more utility, and the end of morality becomes "the greatest happiness of the greatest number." [8]

Thus the three schools of positivism, utilitarianism, and pragmatism tend to coalesce, culminating in an altruistic utilitarianism which sublimates away the ugly implications of positivism and pragmatism while absorbing their more digestible residue. This is not a description of the chronological process but of the end result. In the intellectual climate of contemporary America, particularly that prevailing in university circles, this altruistic utilitarianism, often in a highly refined twentieth century version, represents the dominant component. The outlook of the *New Republic* and the *Nation*, those two periodicals from which so many American liberals derive their thoughts for the week, amounts to little more despite vague Marxian overtones. Social and political scientists may vary considerably in their attitudes on specific issues, but their thinking is likely to

[5] His principal philosophical works are the *Introduction to the Principles of Morals and Legislation*, London, 1789, and Oxford, 1892 (reprinted from the new ed. of 1823); and *Deontology*, London, 1834.
[6] See his *Analysis of the Phenomena of the Human Mind*, London, 1829.
[7] Mill's most important utilitarian writings are *Utilitarianism*, London, 1863, and *An Examination of Sir William Hamilton's Philosophy*, London, 1865. It may be noted that the term "utilitarian," though first popularized by John Stuart Mill, was not—as is commonly believed—coined by him. Bentham had already used it in the same sense; however, it does not appear in James Mill.
[8] For a comprehensive though somewhat dated treatment of the whole English utilitarian school, see Leslie Stephen, *English Utilitarians*, 3 vols., London, 1900. A much briefer and highly sympathetic discussion is Professor William Davidson's *Political Thought: the Utilitarians from Bentham to J. S. Mill*, London and New York, 1902.

be implicitly based on a combination of penchant for the experimental method, applied only to those subjects which have apparent "practical" relevance and workability, for the purpose of bettering the institutional and collective life of man. Such a schema certainly has the advantage of being simple and at the same time superficially adequate; but apart from its lack of complexity, its seeming independence of traditional value-judgments and absolutes often provides the last refuge for the intellectual who wants to hang on to a skeptical philosophy and at the same time avoid admitting that, given certain premises commonly accepted today, power politics is strict logic and might always makes right.

Now it would be difficult to deny that the principle of "the greatest happiness for the greatest number," tempered by a healthy empiricism and spirit of practicality, has inspired certain individuals to noble action, and that those who preached such a code were in the vanguard of progressive thought for more than a hundred years. However, Arthur Koestler's contention that the "greatest happiness" principle is something unique with the nineteenth century, with ethics following the trend of scientific development and philosophic speculation by "adopting a quantitative language," is sheer nonsense.[9] It is an integral part of the traditional Christian social ethic included in the concept of the common good (*bonum commune*). Where then is the great ideological failure of the altruistic utilitarians?

We have seen that the ethical control of power requires both the establishment of satisfactory criteria for its use and of obligation to comply with those criteria. But the modern utilitarian philosophy, even in its most eclectic form, fails not only to provide obligation, but in the last analysis, criteria as well. Certainly the mere method, a synthesis of positivism and

[9] See his *The Yogi and the Commissar*, New York, 1945, p. 222.

pragmatism, does not create obligation toward anything. Nor does the "happiness of the greatest number" principle per se, which in fact does not even constitute a true standard of utility. The essential weakness of this whole school is that it can never bridge the gap between what is useful to the individual and what will make the greatest number happy. Unless he is prepared to make the broad and unjustified assumption that personal interest always coincides with collective interest, the utilitarian who argues with Bentham that "every virtuous act results in a balance of pleasure" (that is, pleasure to the individual),[10] might as well advocate sheer hedonism. The "greatest happiness" principle is something added on for no logical reason at all.

While accepting Bentham's general doctrine,[11] John Stuart Mill sensed this hiatus and tried to bridge it with his famous syllogism, which will long be cited in logic texts as a classic example of the fallacy of composition: Each man should so act as to insure his own happiness; self-happiness of the individual is best insured by the happiness of the race; therefore the individual should act for the happiness of the race to insure his own happiness.[12] But beyond putting bad logic into more "logical" form, Mill actually did not go beyond Bentham at all in his basic justification of utilitarianism. His minor premise is the usual liberal assumption that self-interest coincides with the common interest.

Nor have latter-day utilitarians been able to improve on this position. It is futile to argue that the failure of men and states-

---

[10] *Introduction to the Principles of Morals and Legislation*, p. 72.

[11] Mill, of course, added many refinements, distinguishing between qualitative as well as quantitative pleasures, and differing in his analysis of the moral feeling.

[12] Essentially this fallacy consists in "shifting a term from a distributive to a collective application." See Thomas Crumley, *Logic: Deductive and Inductive*, New York, 1934, pp. 255 ff.

men to glimpse such a basic harmony of interests through the cloud of superficial difference and dispute does not invalidate a morality which demands only that "true" or "enlightened" self-interest coincide with the general interest. The assumption that "enlightened self-interest" always induces to action which is likewise in the interest of the many cannot be empirically justified and can be defended only in terms of higher values which give a special meaning to the adjective "enlightened." But it is precisely these values for which the utilitarians make no provision.

If the basic harmony of secular interests were a reality, then bank robbers and baby killers, or at least highly intelligent amoralists like Goebbels, could be converted by argument alone. But most men realize that no such harmony exists in that material order where they compete one against the other and use whatever power they may possess to gain personally desired objectives. Truly enough, they may refrain from certain action inimical to the welfare of their fellow men for reasons of morality or expediency, and they may often find that what makes for the general welfare also makes for their own welfare, just as they may find they can sometimes achieve certain objectives cooperatively which they cannot achieve alone. But few indeed would be willing to admit that never in their experience has selfish personal advantage been opposed to the welfare of the many.

Professor E. H. Carr has devoted considerable effort and space to analyzing "the colossal paradox of a belief in the harmony of interests," [13] and concludes that "the harmony of interests between nations as a basis of international morality has become no more credible than the harmony of interests between in-

[13] See his *The Twenty Years' Crisis, 1919–1939*, London, 1940, especially Chap. IV. See also his *Conditions of Peace*, London, 1942, pp. 103 ff.

dividuals as a basis of social morality at home." [14] The fact that the development of the atomic bomb and of ever more effective methods of destruction creates an imperative harmony of interests among nations in the preservation of peace is not necessarily of primary importance on the level of actual power use and abuse. While Professor Carr has been unduly harsh to the sincere idealism of the peace movement in contending that the divergent interests of nations with relation to maintenance or change of a given *status quo* are "disguised and falsified by the platitude of a general desire to avoid conflict," [15] it is true that modern instruments of power may tempt an amoral ruler of men to action in hope of achieving victory by one swift stroke which will crush opposition before it is prepared to defend itself, and kill off at the beginning all those usual forces of resistance to oppression which, so often in the past, by patience, endurance, and courage, have finally risen to overthrow a tyranny. Fingers will itch in the predicted age of push-button warfare, as improvements in the techniques of destructive power make the possessor of preponderant power at any given time relatively stronger than he has ever been before.

As long as individual men lust for power and all it brings, and as long as they can attain it by riding roughshod over opposition both within and without the state or other institutions in which they seek or have control, no basic harmony of interests exists between self-interest and the general welfare in a competitive world where the struggle for rank, glory, wealth, and status is an ever-present factor. An unscrupulous ruler may have just as much disregard for the basic welfare of his own country as of other countries, pursuing immediate personal objectives and heedless of long-term results. He may simply

[14] *Conditions of Peace,* p. 107.
[15] *The Twenty Years' Crisis, 1919–1939,* p. 69.

be content to say "après moi, le deluge." But even if he aspire like Hitler to build his form of tyranny for one thousand years, he will be thinking in terms of narrow party and racial interests, certainly not of the happiness of the greatest number.

No theory, therefore, which reduces the motivation for human action to sheer personal or group selfishness can create any obligation to observe unselfish ideals. Utilitarianism fails completely to provide the basis for a stable, just, and orderly society in which power is used according to ethical criteria.

In a sense, of course, any valid normative science, any philosophy which sets up rules for conduct, must be utilitarian; for no rational person advocates a course of action which he knows will not be "useful" toward the end he desires to achieve. But "utility" in a vacuum provides no standard of conduct. As we have noted, the question inevitably arises: Useful for what? A workable utilitarianism must not only assume but must establish some absolute standards of utility; but in so doing it ceases to be utilitarianism in the traditional sense, which attempts to dispense with the concept of moral purpose and to base itself on a supposed harmony of interests between each individual and all other individuals.

A further basic weakness also vitiates the whole approach of the positivist-utilitarian-pragmatist school. Professed metaphysics of course it has none, for its proponents deny that such theorizing is valid or desirable; but its implied epistemology, at the start, eliminates all logical basis for everything which is later advocated. One of the many merits of Professor Sabine's *History of Political Theory* is its recognition of the debt of utilitarian liberalism to David Hume; [16] yet he fails to realize that

[16] See George H. Sabine, *A History of Political Theory*, New York, 1937, p. 598 *passim*. The groundwork, for example, of John Stuart Mill's *System of Logic*, London, 1843, is little more than a reproduction of Hume's epistemology.

any system deriving from the pan-phenomenalism of Hume must end in complete skepticism. That, of course, is a hard truth which few can swallow; in fact Hume could never entirely swallow it himself.[17] But a truth it remains nevertheless. We refer here to "skepticism" as a technical philosophical term, that is, the doctrine that no certain knowledge of reality is possible; and we do not think that any serious student of Hume will today deny that his theory of knowledge leads to precisely such a position. For, as Professor Turner has put it, "He reduced mind as well as matter to mere phenomenon, and denied the ontological nexus between cause and effect. He maintained that there is no permanent, immutable element in the world of our experience, and that there is no valid principle which can justify metaphysical speculation concerning the world beyond our experience." [18]

It is one of the great ironies of philosophic history, a fine example of the epistemological muddle into which empiricism can lead, that the Marxists wage unceasing war against all fol-

[17] Else how explain his later historical and economic writings which certainly posit the truth of our knowledge. Though most of them are probably apocryphal, the numerous anecdotes are significant which have Hume either admitting that his philosophy had led him up a blind alley, or else confiding to a friend that he didn't really mean all he said, anyway, but was just trying to shock people.

[18] *History of Philosophy*, Boston, 1929, pp. 523–524.
Professor Gilson has brilliantly analyzed the Humean epistemology linking it to Malebranchian occasionalism as well as to Lockean empiricism. See his *The Unity of Philosophical Experience*, London, 1938, pp. 218–223. See also for further discussion of Hume: B. M. Laing, *David Hume*, London, 1932; John Laird, *Hume's Philosophy of Human Nature*, London, 1923; Friedrich Hasse, *Das Problem der Gueltigkeit in der Philosophie Humes*, Munich, 1919. Ralph W. Church, *Hume's Theory of the Understanding*, London, 1935.
The pertinent works of Hume himself are: *Enquiry Concerning Human Understanding*, in which he recast the first book of the *Treatise on Human Nature*; and *Enquiry Concerning the Principles of Morals*, in which he recast the third book. See also his *Essays, Moral, Political, and Literary*, Edinburgh, 1742.

lowers of Hume. Yet under different labels, they also claim to
be positivist and pragmatic in method, utilitarian in objective.
Though logically it ought to be, "Communism is emphatically
not a skepticism"; [19] and the Marxists will have nothing to do
with a theory of knowledge which denies all certainty. Lenin
realized that, if the epistemological foundation is weak, the
entire theoretical system built thereon must topple. Hence his
continual attacks on what he calls "Humean agnosticism." As
Professor Etienne Gilson has pointed out, "More than forty
times, in his *Materialism and Empirio-Criticism*, Lenin came
back to this central position in his philosophy, that Hume had
begotten Kant, who in turn had begotten Mill, Mach, Huxley,
Cohen, Renouvier, Poincaré, Duhem, James, and all the exponents" of this agnosticism. [20] He insists that despite the petty
changes "made in the terminology or argument of preceding
systems" all their doctrines add up to the same thing, which is
Humeanism. [21]

Now this Marxist method of confident affirmation, which
superimposes an epistemology of certitude on an impossible
metaphysics, also fails to provide for ethical control of power;
but it does show a keen realization that we must know that we
know before we have a right to talk about ends and means in
the world which we know. One cannot make this point too
often. Most Anglo-American political scientists still continue to

[19] Gilson, *op. cit.*, p. 295.   [20] *Ibid.*, p. 296.
[21] See his *Materialism and Empirio-Criticism*, London, 1927, p. 82; also
pp. 84–85, 133–135, 160–162.
P. Ludas, in his Preface to Engels' *Ludwig Feuerbach and the Outcome
of Classical German Philosophy*, New York, 1935, p. 10, has stated this
viewpoint well: "To this day, all those philosophical tendencies which in
England and the United States parade under the name of 'philosophy,'
such as pragmatism, neo-realism, behaviourism, etc., are admittedly nothing but various shades of agnosticism. But all of them in the final analysis
are rooted in the philosophy of Hume."

favor the positivist-utilitarian-pragmatist approach largely because they have never realized just where such a philosophy must lead them, and fail to appreciate the position at which its modern exponents have arrived. Thus Professor F. C. S. Schiller's attacks on formal logic strike at the validity of the very reasoning process itself, apart from the question of whether our knowledge of the external world is certain.[22] Although already foreshadowed in his *Formal Logic,* published in 1912, this extreme view represents the culmination point in the thinking of a man who, ironically enough, could not escape the "logical" implications of his epistemology. And most ruthlessly logical of all, Hans Vaihinger disdains to use the old pragmatist sophistry that what works is true for our purposes, but merely argues that we must act as if what works were true.[23] His is the last desperate attempt of philosophic skepticism to have its cake and eat it too; but there is nothing left to eat. We are reduced to a philosophical diet of air; and despite all the "as ifs" Professor Vaihinger is able to hypothesize, death from mental malnutrition becomes inevitable. The next step from "as if" can only be complete solipsism. No ethical basis for control of power is to be found in this shadow world of vanished reality. We need not even search. For it simply is not there.

The next time the writer of a learned work blissfully notes in his Preface that he will have nothing to do with philosophy, that he is interested only in hard facts, and does not believe in absolutes but only in the empirical method of trial and error, a healthy pragmatism, it will be well to remember how insubstantial is his epistemological support. A slight application of logic and fantasy will bring him crashing to the ground,

[22] See *The Personalist,* Winter, 1938, p. 19.
[23] Hans Vaihinger, *The Philosophy of "As if,"* trans. C. K. Ogden, London, 1924.

where he may mercifully lie and admire the endless phantasma-
goria of pan-phenomenalism presided over by the kindly shade
of David Hume.

CONTRACTUALISM AND CONSENT

While the classical theories of contractualism have all gone
into discard, they represented, after a somewhat shaky start, a
sincere attempt to establish an ethical basis for state power and
its use, and they have had great influence on our political thinking. Yet the hypothesis of a primary contract as the foundation
of society or the state has left its mark not only as an effort to
explain why power should entail responsibility but as fore-
runner of a concept of collective will which, in our own day,
has provided a convenient argument in the ideology of fascism.

Some eighty-five years ago, Sir Henry Maine wrote that
"the movement of the progressive societies has hitherto been
a movement from status to contract"; [24] but to the contractualists the process was quite the reverse. At first there was apparently neither status nor contract but merely a *state* of
nature; then for one reason or another—depending on the
writer's concept of this natural state [25]—came a general compact, the *contrat social*, from which derived not only the
political state but also whatever rights and duties the individual
has relative to that state.

For many, contractualism is synonomous with Jean Jacques
Rousseau. Yet his was but one form, felicitously phrased and
best integrated into his political philosophy, of a doctrine generally accepted even by men as far apart in goal as Hooker

[24] *Ancient Law*, first published London, 1861, edition of 1907, with introduction and notes by Sir Frederick Pollock, p. 174.
[25] Roughly, contractualists may be divided into those who thought the
state of nature was good (as Rousseau appeared to at times), and those
who thought it was bad (like Hobbes).

and Hobbes.[26] In Thomas Hobbes, the state, the "great Leviathan" and "Martial God," "the Multitude . . . united in One Person," "the Incarnate Self of Everybody," commands nothing more than the obedience of sheer self-advantage, personal utility.[27] His reasoning, for what it is worth, applies exactly the same whether the "Leviathan" comes into existence through the spontaneous, unreflective action of its constituents, or through their deliberate agreement. The contract is something tacked on; it has essentially nothing to do with what Hobbes considers the duty of the individual to the state, which is really a duty of the individual to himself.[28]

The social contract also plays an anomalous role in the political theory of John Locke. Upon close analysis it shrinks into the position of something merely auxiliary to a more basic source of obligation. To Locke the social contract brings great benefits to men, but these are only confirmations or protection of natural rights which men possess apart from the fact that they have contracted to protect them.[29] We shall later see how a distorted version of natural law, deriving from a combination of theories about an original state of nature, "natural" rights in

[26] See for example: John Locke, *Two Treatises on Government*, 1689; Richard Hooker, *The Laws of Ecclesiastical Polity*, published partly in 1594–1597, and partly posthumously; Thomas Hobbes, *The Leviathan*, 1651; Samuel Pufendorf, *De jure naturae et gentium*, reproduction of edition of 1688, trans. by C. H. and W. A. Oldfather, Oxford, 1934.

[27] *Leviathan*, Chap. XVII.

[28] This is the whole implication of his description of human nature in *Leviathan*, Chap. I–XV, especially Chap. XIII; it is the crux of his argument. It is true that Hobbes gives the very words of his hypothetical contract: "I authorise and give up my right of Governing myself, to this Man, or to the Assembly of Men, on this condition, that thow give up thy Right to him, and authorise all his Actions in like manner"—but without ever equating the need for such an actual contract with the reason for observing it which he states. *Diliges te super omnia et alios homines propter te* has no intrinsic connection with the *concursus mentum. Ibid.*, Chap. XVII.

[29] See his *Two Treatises on Government*, Book II, section 25.

such state, and the social contract, has sent many writers on the subject up a blind alley.[30] Suffice it to note here that any ethical obligation to refrain from misuse of power which Locke may claim to establish derives from his theory of natural rights and not from his contractualism, for nowhere does he maintain that the mere act of agreement creates new values. It is merely a means to certain desired ends. Nothing need be said about his sensist and empiricist epistemology, which led directly to Hume's pan-phenomenalism. Many philosophical currents have flown from Locke, most of them muddy; his followers soon realized that his theory of knowledge was completely incompatible with the assertion of natural rights.

Jean Jacques Rousseau, however, attempted to show that obligation could be derived solely from the operation of human wills agreeing to contract, and ended up with the result of this contract completely overwhelming the wills responsible for it. His picture of the nonsocial nature of man, toning down the violently antisocial natural man painted by Hobbes, added a new feature to previous descriptions of the primitive state of nature; [31] but the crux of his approach is in the relationship of the individual will to the so-called general will. To Rousseau there exists no intrinsic need for political society; men freely willed to create the state, and "each individual, anxious to guard his own liberty, while benefiting from the advantages of a collective organization, declared that he would freely give up all his rights to the general will, provided that he himself had

[30] See below, pp. 71 ff.

[31] Just how much Rousseau idealized the state of nature remains a moot question. The picture he paints in the *Social Contract*, Book I, Chap. VIII, is hardly idyllic; but some of his descriptions of primitive man are more sentimentally laudatory. One cannot consider the *Social Contract* without reference to his other writings like *Emile*, in which the "noble savage" is truly noble. See, however, A. J. Carlyle, *Political Liberty*, Oxford, 1941, pp. 182 ff.

his legitimate share in the formation of the general will." [32] The concept of popular sovereignty, which so strongly influenced the ideology of the French Revolution, seemed a logical corollary to this line of reasoning. But Rousseau did not stop with mere argument against the absolute sovereignty of kings and their divine right to abuse power. He went on to claim that "the constant will of all the members of a state, is the general will," that the social whole is a higher moral person than the individual person, and that subservience to the general will really makes the individual will free in that the former truly expresses the universal in human nature. [33]

But it is not apparent why the individual is in any way morally obligated to obey the general will merely because he has "freely and previously accepted" it in the social contract, nor what makes the collectivity a higher moral person, just as it is not apparent what would prevent the general will, identified with "the will of the generality," from abusing power, even though there might be an implied contractual obligation of the new "popular" rulers to act in the general welfare. Value-judgments in a vacuum about the superior worth of the general will are no guarantee against misuse of power or, for that matter, no argument against the individual, ruler or subject, who says that he is here and now interested in satisfying a desire of his particular human nature, whether it be a universal desire or not. There is no merit in universality or in keeping a contract apart from an ethical system that justifies these as values because they tend to achieve the ends of human existence towards which conduct should be ordinated. The obligation of contract is only a moral obligation within the context of a moral code which makes it so.

Historically speaking, it seems clear that the original social

[32] Yves de la Briere, "The Origin of Political Power," *Modern Schoolman,* XII (1935), 52.   [33] *Social Contract,* Book IV, Chap. II.

contract has never existed. John Morley has aptly remarked: "Viewed in the light of 'the observed and recorded experience of mankind,' the ground and origin of society is not a compact, that never existed in any known case, and never was a condition of obligation either in primitive or developed societies, either between subjects or sovereign, or between the equal members of a sovereign body." [34] Yet viewed as a "methodological fiction," the social contract theory does contain a kernel of truth which its exponents have unfortunately buried under a mass of unwarranted supposition and fanciful anthropology. Ernest Barker is somewhat overgenerous in claiming that "the apostles . . . of social contract were not concerned with historical origins. They were thinking not of the chronological antecedents, but of the logical presuppositions of political society. They meant that they could only explain society if they presupposed contracting individuals with individual rights." [35] But he is correct in implying the possibility of a rationale of the social contract theory which cannot be upset by mere historical argument but which "can only be invalidated by a proof either that it fails to explain what it has to explain, or that this can be explained otherwise." [36] Such a rationale would largely assimilate the social contract theory into the consent theory of governmental authority and divorce it from the atomistic implications inherent in the usual contractualist picture of individuals forming the state for essentially negative purposes and not because men are political animals whose personalities can find fullest development only within the state. Even here, however, mere consent has no ethical significance except as a desirable

[34] *Rousseau*, London, 1886, II, 183–184.
[35] Barker, *Political Thought in England from Herbert Spencer to the Present Day*, London and New York, p. 166.
[36] *Ibid.*, pp. 166–167.

method of determining the locus of authority within a larger framework of ends and means.

Unfortunately, Rousseau's introduction of a new unifying and positive factor into contractualist theory opened the way to an ever more aberrant development. What began as largely an attempt to establish the moral character of public authority changed into an elaborate argument for absolute state dominion over individual men and eventually provided one of the conceptual foundations of modern totalitarianism. Although it is true that Hobbes and Spinoza used their versions of the social contract in defense of absolutism, most of the early contractualists such as Althusius, Locke, Grotius, and Pufendorf stressed the "moral limitations on rulers." [37] But Rousseau's concept of the general will lent itself readily to the complete Hegelian subordination of the individual to the state. In an effort, perhaps, to bridge the logical hiatus between the general will and the obligation of the individual to conform to that general will, Rousseau indulged in vague distinctions between the real will and the apparent will which, in the hands of a Neo-Hegelian like Bosanquet, were to be rationalized into the absurd and dangerous theory of the unconscious real will. This "real will" of society which the state enforces is supposed to represent what each individual would desire if he were perfectly developed in both intelligence and morality.[38] The absolutist implications of any theory that ascribes moral infallibility to the state and justifies the use of power on that basis should be apparent. It is true that "we can only justify ourselves and we

[37] "The real emphasis of the theory was that law and government fall within the general field of morals; they are not merely expressions of force but are properly subject to ethical criticism." George H. Sabine, *op. cit.*, p. 431.
[38] See Bernard Bosanquet, *The Philosophical Theory of the State*, London, 1899, Chapters IX–X.

can only justify the State which is part of ourselves and *is* ourselves, if, in some such way as Green and Bosanquet suggest, we believe that the self and its individuality are asserted in and through society, and that morality is something affirmative, something in which we affirm our whole selves, and not something in which we deny one half of our nature"; [39] nevertheless, this is far from imputing, as did Bosanquet, complete righteousness to the state in the use of power on the actual operating level. The ramifications of nineteenth century Hegelian idealism and its effects on political thought are too complex for discussion here,[40] but it may be noted that Nazi and Fascist theorists were quick to seize upon the doctrine of the "real will" as an argument for totalitarianism, to which they, of course, added Nietzschean, racist, nihilist, and dynamist trimmings.[41]

Despite the absolutist implications which have been read into it, a realistic theory of the state must recognize a legitimate use for the concept of the general will. But in such use it is merely descriptive of a process and a fact, and has no direct

[39] Ernest Barker, *op. cit.*, p. 141.
[40] See L. T. Hobhouse, *The Metaphysical Theory of the State*, London, 1918, for a searching discussion and criticism of this whole school. Closely allied to the Hegelian idealist concept of the state is the concept of the state as an organism. Dr. Francis Coker's *Organismic Theory of the State*, New York, 1910, is the standard treatise in English on the subject. For a new and sympathetic interpretation of Hegel's philosophy of history, however, see Prince Hubertus zu Loewenstein, *The Germans in History*, New York, 1946, pp. 227-240.
[41] See Walther R. Darré, *Das Bauerntum als Lebensquell der Nordischen Rasse*, Leipzig, 1929, p. 287; Roberto Farinacci, "Render unto Caesar" (trans. from *Regina Fascista*, Cremona); *Living Age*, January, 1939, p. 410; Giovanni Gentile, *The Reform of Education*, London, 1922, pp. 29-32; *Che Cosa è il Fascismo*, Florence, 1925, pp. 235-236; Benito Mussolini, *The Doctrine of Fascism*, Florence, 1936, p. 57; Alfredo Rocco, "The Political Doctrine of Fascism," *International Conciliation*, October, 1926, pp. 402-403; Alfred Rosenberg, *Der Mythus des 20. Jahrhunderts*, Berlin, 1935 ed., p. 2; *Blut und Ehre*, Berlin, 1936, p. 246.

relation to the morality of power. Underlying any state which is not based on sheer tyranny there must be a foundation of common consent which unites those opposed to a specific policy or party in power to those who favor such party or policy. It is the will for the continuance of the associational framework which constitutes a specific state in broadest definition, the "popular support for the fundamental law" of the state "itself which is greater than any narrow or transient majority." [42]

The existence of this general will provides no guarantee against the abuse of power; it may in the case of a popularly supported dictatorship simply provide more power to be abused. As we have already indicated, the mere fact of consent does not create morality; to this it is related only in terms of other criteria which may make majority consent, for example, desirable as the basis of action affecting a group. The concept of the general will on a foundational level is helpful in explaining the conditions under which power operates in the state, but we must seek elsewhere for the source of those standards and the obligation to observe them which are essential to the ethical control of power.

THE LACUNAE OF LEGALISM

A hyberbolic cynic once remarked that "in the last analysis every theory of the law turns out to be a reasoned case for law-

[42] Robert M. MacIver, *Leviathan and the People*, Baton Rouge, La., 1939, p. 150. The most intelligent treatment of this whole question of the general will is to be found in various political writings of Professor MacIver. See especially his *The Modern State*, Oxford, 1926, pp. 8, 193 ff., 447 ff., 487 ff.

However, his statement that "in the modern world every system of government must rest on the general consent of the mass of the people" (*Leviathan and the People*, p. 87) raises a question as to whether, with improving techniques of power and coercion, a government cannot seize power and maintain control through terror, only gradually strengthening its position through a monopoly of propaganda until a sort of factitious consent is created.

lessness." While it would not be strictly accurate to claim that an examination of modern legal theory strikingly confirms this generalization, it is no exaggeration to say that such theory woefully fails to come to grips with the essential problem of power, the prevention of the abuse of which is a primary function of law. Yet much of the thought given in recent decades to the control of power has been concentrated on the development of legal formulae and institutions, without apparent realization of the inadequacy of legal theory to establish any obligation towards those norms of law which would prohibit the abuse of power. International law, the subject matter of which impinges, or ought to impinge, directly on the area in which states exercise their power in relation to other states, is left devoid of that theoretical foundation which alone can make its observance a requirement of ethics.

Many international lawyers, especially those steeped in the Anglo-American tradition, even today tend to pass over this question with some remark about the sterility of metaphysical discussion. The discussion may sometimes be sterile, but the issues are vital. Ignoring them solves nothing and indicates only a failure to recognize essentials.

Contemporary legal theory, such as it is, has been largely influenced by two nineteenth century approaches to the law, the historical and the analytical, both of which shared with the earlier naturalist approach the common characteristic of being non-creative.[43] Sterility came not from lack of talented advocates, but from lack of a vital philosophy to advocate. In the field of international law this non-creative outlook was so dominant that jurists ceased almost entirely to lead the way in

[43] One of Dean Roscoe Pound's contributions has been to point out this hiatus in creative legal theory, though some not converted to "sociological jurisprudence" may prefer the word "breakdown" in place of "hiatus." See his *Law and Morals*, Chapel Hill, N.C., 1926, pp. 33 ff.

advocating new principles for new situations, but merely recorded those which states were content to accept and pay damages for violating. After depicting the law purely in terms of its existent positive self, they left it there with perhaps a reluctant admission that a rule was bad, too bad, but nevertheless the rule.

Nominal followers of a great tradition, the naturalists had preserved little more than the old deductive method, reasoning from accepted premises, or from vague general concepts like sovereignty, to more or less inflexible conclusions. They adopted Pufendorf's concept of a law supposed to be binding upon men in the primitive state of nature, of rights which these men carried into society with them when they made the social compact, and used it largely as an argument in justification of the *status quo*.[44] It is not unfair to say that the naturalist approach made scarcely a progressive ripple on the main current of nineteenth century legal thought, but that it helped greatly to contribute to that general misconception of the traditional natural law which still prevails.

The historical school provides a classic example of a good idea put to a bad use. In a sense, both positive international law and municipal law must emphasize history. Without precedent and rules established in the past, there can be no certainty. But it is a distorted viewpoint which makes legal systems merely exemplifications of the working out of historical forces. Under the long shadow of Hegel,[45] writers on jurisprudence like Savigny and Maine described law as an unfolding or realizing

[44] The much-abused theory of "vested rights," so influential in the development of American constitutional law, was a choice fruit. See Edward S. Corwin, "A Basic Doctrine of American Constitutional Law," *Michigan Law Review*, XII (1914), 247.
[45] See especially his *Philosophy of Right*, trans. by S. W. Dyde, London, 1896.

of the idea of right, which expresses itself in the "spirit of the people." [46] In turn, this "spirit of the people crystallizes itself in habit or custom. The inevitable conclusion was that, since law unfolds by its own inner power as part of the dialectical movement of history, the task of the jurist, the judge, is merely to "recognize" the law. Relativism of values and a sort of legal fatalism or ultraconservatism were the logical results of any such attempt to link legal development strictly to the historical dialectic.

Led by John Austin, the analytical school broke away completely from philosophy and ethics. Jurists were to concentrate on "the pure fact of law," and the "pure fact" was the actual fact.[47] A vast accumulation of fine distinctions, of increasingly detailed applications of accepted principles, of criticism of existing law in terms of existing law, began to pile up; and no one will deny the contributions of the analytical school to precision and clarity within the field of municipal law. As basis of Austin's narrow approach was his "command theory" of law, which went back to the old notion of rules handed down from on high—but failed to look very high for their source. A "determinate human superior" was necessary and ample to make law, but no criteria of superiority were provided. Assuming the definition, international law amounted to sheer misnomer, mere morality at best, and so Austin disposed of it.

But mere morality or not, the limited rules of international law remained; and it was not long before jurists began to feel Austin's excision too clean-cut. Late nineteenth century legal positivists like Holland, Liszt, and Oppenheim found themselves

[46] See Friedrich Savigny, *System des heutigen römischen Rechts*, Leipzig, 1840; and Sir Henry Maine, *Ancient Law*, London, 1861, and *Early History of Institutions*, London, 1871.
[47] See John Austin, *Lectures on Jurisprudence*, Campbell's 5th ed., London, 1911, for the classical statement of the analytical approach.

able to accept international law as law by application of the so-called "consent theory." International law was "law between states, not above states," [48] based on contract not statute. The troublesome problem of withdrawal of consent was, however, never thoroughly worked out, even though it is the crux of any consent theory of law. For if state consent is the causal factor in making international law true law, then how, once that causal factor is withdrawn, can the law remain?

By the turn of the century, the strictly positivist approach of analytical jurisprudence had found its logical terminus in the principle enunciated by Professor Dicey that "the law of every country, as for example of England, or of Italy, consists of all the principles, rules, or maxims enforced by the courts of that country as being supported by the authority of the state." [49] While this may have been a realistic description of operative law, it marked in spirit the complete subordination of legal philosophy to the lawyer and the judge. From criticizing the natural law school for its unconscious subjectivity, the positivists had come to assert a subjective source as the very essence of law itself. The influence of Diceyan "judicialism" on international thought prior to 1914 was considerable, expressing itself in the widespread belief that the creation of an international court with compulsory jurisdiction would solve all the problems of world politics and result in the control of power through judicial injunction. [50] Thus the attempt to exclude theory from

[48] Lassa Oppenheim, *International Law*, 2d ed., London, 1912, p. 5. See also Sir Thomas Holland, *Lectures on International Law*, London, 10th ed., 1933, especially Chap. I.
[49] See his famous article, "Private International Law as a Branch of the Law of England," *Law Quarterly Review*, VI (1899), 3.
[50] See Sir Alfred Zimmern, *The League of Nations and the Rule of Law 1918–1935*, London, 1936, Part I, Chap. XI, for a keen and critical discussion of this movement.

jurisprudence ended with a complete divorce from those basic workaday realities in which positivism exulted.

If Anglo-American jurists rejected theory and identified law with institutions and men, continental jurists, particularly the Germans, went to the other extreme of subordinating all institutions and men to a single theory. Starting with the concept of unlimited state sovereignty, which was likewise generally admitted by the positivists, German legal writers of the Hegelian school made short shrift of the law of nations.[51] With ruthless logic, they pointed out that a consent theory of law implied that, with consent lacking, there was no law. Hence Professor Lasson could write that the state "is unbounded and unlimited with regard to everything outside itself. . . . It is an unbridled will of selfishness";[52] and Professor Jellinek, that "whenever the observance of international law is found to be in conflict with the existence of the State, the rule of law retires to the background, because the State is put higher than any particular rule of law. . . . International law exists for the State and not the State for International law."[53] Unable to realize that these were reasonable deductions from the premises they themselves espoused, Anglo-American legal positivists were shocked into instinctive reaction against such international anarchy, but in

[51] There is, of course, far more to Hegelian political theory than mere decoration for a legal fiction of sovereignty. With the state conceived as the realization of the moral idea, as the "march of God in the world," and its nature and constituency pictured in organic terms, sovereignty as a concept takes on entirely new connotations. If the state constitutes an absolute value in itself, obviously the only international law which need be obeyed is that which makes for the self-preservation and development of the state—and then not because it is law. See Hegel's *Grundlinien der Philosophie des Rechts*, in *Saemtliche Werke*, VI, Section 258, Eng. trans. by S. W. Dyde, London, 1896.

[52] *Prinzip und Zukunft des Voelkerrechts*, Berlin, 1871, p. 22.

[53] *Allgemeine Staatslehre*, 2d ed., Berlin, 1905, p. 377.

rebuttal were able to offer nothing more than a moral protest completely lacking theoretical foundation.

At the end of the second decade of this century, the theory of law, and of international law in particular, stood in a bad way. Not only did the latter fail to provide any basis for the control of state power, but the basic assumptions of its various exponents could actually be used as justification for almost any abuse of power. In the hazy optimism of the period just after World War I, Anglo-American international lawyers were content to remain philosophically asleep because their dreams seemed very pleasant indeed; but on the Continent a new vitality of theoretical discussion was noticeable among the jurists. Reacting against the modified consent theory of the so-called dualist school deriving from Professor Triepel,[54] followers of the Vienna School espoused a theory of legal "monism" and generally asserted the supremacy of international law in the hierarchy of legal norms, although in turn failing to achieve that satisfactory synthesis of ethics and law which is the essential basis for the recognition of such supremacy.

After a critical analysis of Triepel's theory of the *Vereinbarung* (agreement) which would base international law on the irrevocable consent of states but fails to provide any conclusive reason why such consent should be irrevocable, Dr. Hans Kelsen develops his concept of the pure legal science (*reine Rechtslehre*).[55] This involves no denial of the relation

[54] See his *Voelkerrecht und Landesrecht*, Berlin, 1899, for a comprehensive statement of the dualist position. Legal dualism sharply distinguishes municipal law from international law and makes them essentially different in kind.

[55] The analysis attempted here is a very inadequate summary of an extremely involved series of arguments appearing in a number of works and perhaps most fully set forth in Kelsen's *General Theory of Law and State*, an English edition of which was published by the Harvard University Press in 1945.

between ethics, politics, sociology, and law, but requires a clear distinction between them and jurisprudence. For the study of law is a science in its own right, inasmuch as it is a mode of cognition. Granting this definition, the argument for strict legal monism follows inexorably. Since that unity of cognition which is characteristic of a science requires unity of object, the object of legal science—law—must likewise be a unity. Any dualistic theory of the law must accordingly deny the legality of the law of nations.

But law is essentially a normative science embodied in a code regulative of conduct, and Kelsen reasons that there must be a hierarchy of norms each unit of which is based upon another to which it is logically related. His analysis leads to one fundamental norm (the *Grundnorm*), which is the source and foundation of all law and a necessary postulate, since legal norms are explicable only by other norms from which they derive existence. But the jurist cannot venture further than the conclusion that some such basic norm must exist, for the ultimate origins of law are determined by so-called "metajuridical considerations."

While this highly integrated jurisprudence of Professor Kelsen throws clarifying light on the necessary and intimate relationship between the various types of law, and provides an apparatus of logical analysis by which to evaluate the structural consistency of legal systems, the final impression which he leaves is one of uncertainty. He seems to lead us up to the door and then reluctantly tell us he has forgotten the key. Without these "metajuridical considerations" it is not even possible to prove the theoretical supremacy of international law over municipal law.[56] Other members of the Vienna School like Professors

[56] A fact which Kelsen plainly admits in his *General Theory of Law and State*, p. 387.

Verdross [57] and Kunz [58] were not satisfied to halt at this point, but have insisted more specifically on the supremacy of the international juridical order as a logical *corollary* of legal monism. But in the last analysis, they likewise have failed to establish any rational basis for such a contention within the limits of purely legal discussion.

Thus the attempt of the Vienna School to establish a "pure legal science," like all attempts to isolate the law from political theory and general philosophy, has merely underlined the impossibility of establishing a truly creative jurisprudence in a vacuum. Perhaps the most suggestive commentary on how little the necessary relation between ethics, metaphysics, and law has been realized by these jurists is their use of the terms monism and dualism. Confusion is inherent in their loose adaptation of traditional philosophic terminology, since the legal monist, in such basic philosophy as he may have, is much more likely to be a philosophical dualist than the legal dualist, who in turn is more likely to be a philosophical monist.

One further post-1918 approach to international law, which may well be called *communitarianism*, deserves consideration. It is inspired by sentiments which all men of good will share, and yet, like so many other well-intentioned modern credos, lacks a valid theoretical foundation for those premises which are essential to its conclusions. As a functional approach defining international law in terms of the need which it fills in a world community of interrelated and mutually dependent states, this *communitarianism* might seem to provide the rationale for a new international legal order; yet closer scrutiny reveals that it begs the essential question.

When Professor A. L. Goodhart writes, "By a society or a

[57] See his *Die Anerkennung Der Staaten und Regierung im Voelkerrecht,* Vienna, 1928.
[58] See his article, "The Vienna School and International Law," *New York University Law Review,* XI (1935), 370.

community we mean that men are in a certain relationship to each other because through that relationship they hope to achieve certain ends," [59] or when Sir Frederick Pollock insists that "the only essential conditions for the existence of law and legal institutions are the existence of a political community and the recognition by its members of settled rules binding upon them in that capacity" [60]—they are merely saying that if such and such conditions exist, then the international community is a reality and the rule of law within it a possibility. Now the existence of at least a limited international community, no matter how dimly reflected in actual practice, can be proved through analysis of the facts of interstate relationship. But that individual men or states have any obligation to act in its interests cannot be established by purely factual analysis or legal argument. At this point the *communitarian* may take refuge in the passive paraphrastic of a Latin proverb: *Voluntas civitatis maximae est servanda;* [61] but this, like that other favorite of the international lawyers, *Pacta sunt servanda,* [62] is merely a conclusion and not a whole argument. The legal mind often cannot seem to grasp that a bare principle does not have the inevitability of a syllogism unless preceded by a major and a minor premise.

It may be argued that states must be subject to law or the international community will perish, since "The laws of a society are . . . those rules of conduct on which the existence of the society is based and the violation of which, in consequence, tends to invalidate the existence of the society." [63] But here again a value is assumed—the international community—which can only be established as such in terms of ethical theory.

---

[59] "Nature of International Law," *Grotius Society Transactions,* XXII (1937), 31.
[60] *First Book in Jurisprudence,* London, 1904, p. 334.
[61] Literally, "The will of the greatest state ought to be observed"; i.e., the will of the international community.
[62] "Treaties ought to be observed."   [63] A. L. Goodhart, *op. cit.,* p. 40.

Within the context of a valid ethical system, the concept of international community does assume prime importance. Yet against those who would shatter this community, or seek the dominance of one state over its other constituent parts, the average *communitarian* can essentially plead only pragmatic utility.[64] Nothing further need be said at this point about the worth of the utilitarian argument; it is no stronger a basis for an international legal code than for political ethics.

It should be clear that modern legal theory suffers from the same fundamental deficiency as political theory, and that unrealized implications likewise hang heavily over the heads of jurists. Positivist jurisprudence has no more validity than positivist political theory, and invites the same abuse of power by those who can profit by it. A primary role of law in the control of power is to provide criteria of conduct the breach of which will bring into action institutional modes of enforcement. But such modes of enforcement may not exist, particularly in the international sphere; or individuals and parties like Hitler and the Nazis may set themselves above and become more powerful than the established law; or the law may be bad and tyrannical to begin with. Law is not sufficient unto itself. Like politics it must be grounded in ethics, and its rules must possess moral sanction. A jurisprudence which does not leave room for such ethical foundation and sanction, which may, in fact, involve certain assumptions and principles incompatible with them, fails to cope with its most pressing problems.

[64] In his *The Function of Law in the International Community*, Oxford, 1933, Professor Hersh Lauterpacht eloquently defended the *communitarian* position, but went further than most in recognizing the need for moral sanction. He apparently failed, however, to appreciate fully what its establishment requires. In his *An International Bill of the Rights of Man*, New York, 1945, he emerges as a proponent of the natural law concept and comes close, in certain respects, to the position advocated in Section II of this book.

IV

The Search for Valid Theory

WE HAVE SEEN that modern attempts to establish criteria for the control of power have failed both in theory and practice because they lack a valid ethical basis. Mere utility, mere consent, or mere legalism, no matter how cleverly disguised or refined, cannot provide obligation to observe any standard which requires more than the furtherance of purely selfish interests. At a time when men need strong principles with strong foundations that will demand assent, the prevailing political and legal philosophies have nothing more to offer than a series of rationalizations, which either ignore essential issues entirely or involve certain assumptions the implications of which are disastrous for the ordination of power in the general welfare.

It is true that certain writers on public affairs have increasingly come to realize the necessity for a new moral purpose in politics, and have been willing frankly to admit the fact and call things by their familiar names. This does not represent merely a greater vociferousness on the part of those who still adhere openly to the traditional Christian values. A gloomy and realistic socialist like Arthur Koestler and a distinguished student of international affairs like Professor E. H. Carr have both come to the conclusion that, without such recovery of moral purpose, "there seems to be no reasonable hope of preventing the destruction of . . . civilisation, either by total war's successor Absolute

War, or by Byzantine conquest—within the next few decades." [1]

But recognition of a need does not always imply the ability to satisfy it. Truly, "pious exhortations are not enough," yet it adds essentially very little to say that "to recover the lost half of our personalities, man's wholeness and holiness, the art and science of contemplation has to be learned; and in order to be learned, it has to be taught." [2] Contemplation is a means to truth, not a guarantee that it will be attained. The reestablishment of moral standards depends on more than the mere fact of contemplation; it requires the achievement of valid and coherent ethical theory integrated into a general system of values. The building of "oases" of moderation and clear thinking by men of good will recommended by Koestler for the "interregnum desert" of the next few decades of chaos and power-abuse, before the birth of a new age,[3] may be a far-sighted counsel, but it provides no index as to the content of good will or as to the reason why men should have good will to begin with.[4]

While much more specific than Koestler, Professor Carr like-wise fails to arrive at any satisfactory basis for that moral purpose which he finds so necessary. In outlining "the conditions which must be fulfilled by any movement or creed likely to make a widespread appeal to the contemporary world and to provide the sense of a common purpose essential to the survival of civilisation," [5] he does little more than state certain broad ethical precepts which should be incorporated into the new

[1] Arthur Koestler, *The Yogi and the Commissar*, New York, 1945, p. 247.
[2] *Ibid.*, p. 246.   [3] *Ibid.*, pp. 100 ff.
[4] If Mr. Koestler's play, *Twilight Bar*, published in New York late in 1945 but apparently finished in 1944, is any indication of his trend of thought, then the net result of all his soul-searching promises to be just another form of that desperate hedonism which failed during the 1920s and every other time it has been tried as the basis of the good society. His oases turn out to be little more than glorified harems.
[5] *Conditions of Peace*, London, 1942, p. 118.

morality and certain political and social problems with which the new morality must cope. He does not discuss the problem of the source of moral obligation, nor does he apparently appreciate that such obligation and the ethical system of which it is a part can only be built on a foundation of valid philosophy.

Despite the sincere groping for solutions in our time, there remains too little recognition of the actual prerequisites of a workable political morality. Too often the search for valid theory moves only on a single level without attempt at integration within the complete structure of human thought and activity. If an ethical system to be effective requires both clear standards and recognition of obligation to observe them, the modern man of intelligence will require, before giving his allegiance, that such standards not only be consistent one with the other but that they derive value from their role in a coherent world scheme, or what the Germans call *Weltanschauung*.

All ethical systems may ultimately be divided into those of conditionate morality and those of absolute morality.[6] The advocate of conditionate morality seeks his standard of conduct in some variable factor such as subjective satisfaction, personal well-being, or personal utility. On the other hand, the advocate of absolute morality finds his standard of conduct in an impersonal norm universally applicable under the same circumstances, a norm which does not vary with individual mood or utility. Only the latter, it should be clear, can provide any sort of basis for the ethical control of power. The various efforts to establish norms of conduct discussed in a previous chapter, camouflaged as some of them may be, fail because they end logically in a completely conditionate morality.

No attempt can be made here to analyze complete systems of

[6] Cf. T. V. Moore, *A Historical Introduction to Ethics*, New York, 1915, pp. 6 ff.

philosophy in all their ramifications and subtleties, or even to catalogue the various theories which men have advanced to explain the nature of reality and the ethical implications of those theories. Some of these, such as the existentialism of Heidegger, make no pretense at the establishment of moral criteria for the control of power. Others, like the monistic idealism of the Hegelians with their false analogy of the organismic state, can be used to justify a tyranny of power. Still others, like the superman philosophy of Nietzsche, actually do justify the ethically uncontrolled use of power by the strong. The contribution of such thinking to totalitarian theory will not be overlooked by the causally percipient. With the collapse of that positivistic utilitarianism basic to liberal thought of the past hundred and twenty years, which, at one time, had seemingly solved the problem of power, the way was ideologically open for men strong and ruthless enough to apply literally these philosophies of uncontrolled power.

Certain concepts and principles may, therefore, clearly be recognized as incompatible with the ethical control of power. On the other hand, there are also certain broad epistemological, psychological, and axiological concepts and principles prerequisite to such control; and it is precisely because they espoused philosophies which left no room for these that so many well-meaning liberals have ended in a moral impasse. To possess validity, an ethical system must begin by assuming the possibility of certain human knowledge of objective truth, the freedom of the human will, and the unique value of the individual human person. Although it is still fashionable to do so, the political theorist gains little and loses much by refusing to discuss these necessary assumptions and by dismissing them airily as the subject of other and more esoteric studies. They are of basic importance to politics, and the attitude taken towards them should logically determine one's entire political philosophy. Their truth can be denied, but then the implications of that denial must be squarely faced.

An affirmative answer to the question, "Can we know anything with certitude?" must be the starting point of all speculative thought for which the thinker claims any validity. A sound theory of knowledge, explicit or implicit, is the necessary beginning of wisdom. The great epistemological debate has been in progress for nearly three thousand years, and the issues are clear, although in each generation there are those who insist on confusing them. As opposed to the skeptics, the traditional philosophic realist makes no absurd claim that all knowledge is certain, or even that most knowledge is certain. He claims only that at times, under specific conditions, men can be certain that their knowledge about some things, including non-mental objects, is certain.[7] Denial of this possibility means denial of the validity of any positive conclusions about ethics, politics, or anything else. Universal doubt leads logically to universal moral anarchy. The very concept of standards and of obligation towards them becomes absurd. No matter how disguised and sugar-coated, the implications of such essentially skeptical modern philosophies as pragmatism or the instrumentalism of Professor Dewey are basically amoral.[8]

While a form of skepticism has found many supporters among faculty members of American law schools,[9] it has as yet had

[7] For an acute and concise analysis of the various historical theories of knowledge and statement of the realist case, see D. J. B. Hawkins, *The Criticism of Experience*, London, 1945.

[8] See above, pp. 33 ff., for a discussion of Hume's panphenomenalistic scepticism and its relation to modern pragmatism.

[9] Strangely enough, this school of jurisprudence which attempts illogically to combine a psychological, experimental, and skeptical approach has taken the name of *realism*, although in animus and implication it runs counter to traditional realism. See Karl Llewellyn, "Some Realism about

little practical effect on the major assumptions of the law, including the possibility of certitude. The entire structure of modern legal process, so essential to the maintenance of liberty and right in the West, is based on the premise that, given adequate evidence, the truth can be ascertained. Universal doubt has no place in the courts. Even in the international sphere, where the rule of law is still so tenuous, no state has yet offered epistemological skepticism as excuse for its transgressions. It is rather difficult to imagine the agent for a defendant state, charged with denying justice to an alien, arguing before an international claims commission: "My government pleads complete non-responsibility. The epistemological viewpoint of the present prime minister and foreign minister can lead to no other conclusion. They do not believe that men can know anything with certitude. They are not certain that any action was taken towards any alien. In fact, they are not certain that my government drew up any *compromis*, or that any claims commission exists. Nor, for that matter, can you be certain of anything, even that I am pleading before you. Nothing is certain. How therefore judge of anything?"

Such a plea is obviously absurd, but no more absurd than the implications of universal doubt in any sphere. Yet many modern thinkers, including perhaps a few philosophically inclined foreign ministers, have defended precisely such universal doubt on the level of theory if not practice. A good example is Lord Balfour whose philosophy logically led to skepticism,[10] but who during his period at the Foreign Office conducted British policy with a fine appreciation of lasting realities. No law, no

---

Realism," *Harvard Law Review*, XLIV (1931), 1237; Jerome Frank, *Law and the Modern Mind*, New York, 1931; Edward S. Robinson, *Law and the Lawyers*, New York, 1935.
[10] See his *A Defense of Philosophic Doubt*, London, 1879.

activity, not even life itself, can continue on the basis of complete uncertainty; and the twentieth century world, threatened by power in the hands of unprincipled men certain of their concrete objectives and ruthless in achieving them, can ill afford the luxury of an epistemology which vitiates at the outset every noble ideal and purpose, and denies inner consistency to any scheme of ethical values attempting to ordinate the use of power. The possibility of certain knowledge of truth has been discussed in thousands of volumes, and it is our conviction that such possibility is a fact, not merely because it is necessary to all rational activity, but because it follows ineluctably from thoughtful consideration of the nature of truth and the process of knowledge. To those who would deny the possibility of certitude, it can only be said that, while they may be entitled to their point of view, they are definitely not entitled to the privilege of feeling moral indignation at evil and abuse of power which they cannot be sure ever took place, or which, if it did take place, cannot be called either right or wrong since they cannot be sure there is a distinction between right and wrong or that anything specifically is ever right or wrong.

If certitude is possible, then such certitude can be expressed in words. Concepts need not forever remain merely conceptual and unexpressed, but this is far from saying that every verbalization necessarily conveys a clear concept or from denying that many words carry with them irrational or emotional connotations which distort meanings. The recent emphasis on semantics has thrown considerable light on the problem of definition,[11] but mere linguistic analysis is not a complete criticism of experience, and the very attempt at such analysis implies that

[11] The classic treatises on semantics remain O. R. Ogden's and I. A. Richard's *The Meaning of Meaning*, New York, 1927, and Alfred Korzybski's *Science and Sanity*, New York, 1933.

words, carefully and rationally chosen, can truly represent correct meanings.

The second necessary assumption of a valid ethical system, as we have noted, is a psychological one—freedom of the human will, the self-determination of action. At a later point, in connection with our discussion of liberty and the power of authority, it will be pertinent to say more about certain positive aspects of volition.[12] Suffice it to note here that, without human freedom of choice, no basis remains for any control of power other than the imposition of superior power. If men can never freely choose their own actions, if everything they do is absolutely conditioned by factors beyond their control, then the whole structure of imperatives established by moral code and positive law loses meaning. Determinism implies not only that individuals deceive themselves when they think they have free choice, but that society and the human relations which take place within it involve a tremendous lie. For fundamental to the approach of man to man in business, in sport, in politics, and in every other phase of normal activity, is the postulate that men are free to make certain decisions and are personally responsible for those decisions.

If the establishment of the rule of law in the political sphere is the condition of peace and the control of power, then room must be left in theory for those voluntaristic concepts which are interwoven into the very fabric of operational law as we know it. A strictly deterministic psychology, be it behavioristic, Freudian, or glandular,[13] is incompatible with any meaningful use of such basic terms as responsibility, intent, negligence, and motive.

[12] See below, pp. 148 ff.
[13] See Mortimer Adler, *What Man Has Made of Man*, New York, 1937, especially pp. 124 ff., for a discerning analysis of the intellectual malaise which the constant flux of these various "isms" and fads indicates.

How absurd, how "unjust," how "immoral," to condemn and punish men, or even to hold them in any way responsible, if they cannot ever help doing what they do! But there can then be no real use of the terms "morality" and "justice"; the judge is fully as irresponsible in his decision as the defendant in his action. The nonsense to which determinism leads in the legal sphere is a forceful *reductio ad absurdum*. If a foreign ambassador were lynched by a mob led by the President of the United States riding a white horse, with the Vice President right behind him, no one could blame this country or hold it responsible since the whole incident, as well as every other incident, would be determined by glands, reflexes, subconscious urges, or some other non-volitional factor.

Similarly, legal intent cannot be present within any significant meaning of the term when conduct is fully predetermined. Ability freely to choose a course of action before attempting to carry it out is essential to that purposeful pursuit of an objective the presence or absence of which we consider closely linked to the question of responsibility.[14]

All of this may seem like belaboring the obvious—yet men persist in advocating the control of power in one breath and determinism in the other. If conduct is really determined, no

[14] A classic judicial formulation of the relation between intent and free will is found in *Oregon-Washington R. & Nav. Co. v. United States* (1913), 205 Fed. 337: "The carrier who knowingly and willfully fails to comply with the provisions of the act is amenable thereto, and in the present case it was incumbent upon the government to show by testimony sufficient to go to the jury that the defendant did so knowingly and willingly fail to unload the hogs within the period of thirty-six hours. The words 'knowingly' and 'willfully' as employed in this act, have been many times construed and their meaning determined. 'Knowingly' signifies 'with a knowledge of the facts' which, taken together, constitute a failure to comply with the statute; and 'willfully' means 'purposely or obstinately' and is designed to describe the attitude of a carrier, who having a free will or choice, either intentionally disregards the statute or is plainly indifferent to its requirements."

matter what happens, it will always be beyond the capacity of men to change; and any hope of purposeful change and improvement is sheer illusion. What men do or fail to do, they do or fail to do because of factors beyond their control, inevitable processes which they can neither deliberately affect or modify. To remain a determinist, one must logically be resigned, not to a lawless world, but to a world wherein physical law is so extensively applicable, so ironclad, that legality becomes meaningless and every destructive activity, every tyranny of power, merely a manifestation of physical law.

The third necessary assumption of an ethics to control power—the unique value of the individual human person—should be more or less self-evident. Unless the individual has value in terms of an accepted and coherent philosophy,[15] there is absolutely no moral reason why superior power should not ride roughshod without regard for effect other than the enhancement of power. Men can deny that man as such has any significance, but they should then be prepared to face the implications of that denial. Right and wrong lose all conventional meaning and there can be no morality of conduct toward individuals. Nor can any mere collectivity of worthless men acquire significance merely because they are a collectivity. Zero plus zero plus zero equals zero. A coherent theory of the common good demands attribution of value to each person that comprises the commonweal, even though that common good may, in cases of conflict, require the subordination of one man's right to that of another.[16]

The idea of individual worth has generally found approval among liberals, even though liberalism originally erred in adopting too atomistic a conception of the individual. But as a value-

[15] See below, pp. 78 ff., 150 ff., for a discussion of certain aspects of individual worth.   [16] See below, pp. 123 ff.

judgment, this viewpoint was often incompatible with other propositions regarding the nature of man and of reality that were espoused at the same time. The curse of unrealized implications which vitiated liberal thought thus attained its fulfillment in those ruthless modern philosophies of action which lead to the complete disregard of individual worth.

The search for valid theory is not, of course, merely a search for an over-all theory which will be internally consistent but also for one which is firmly grounded in a true appraisal of reality. It is the contention of this book that such a theory is possible, and may be found in the traditional concept of the natural law, revitalized and cleansed from the dross of misrepresentation. There are in it long-unused sources of strength and renewal upon which Western political philosophy may draw. As the exposition which follows is intended to make clear, acceptance of natural law does not involve repudiation of reason and common sense but is entirely compatible with their soundest conclusions. In subsequent chapters, we shall attempt to show the concrete application of natural law theory to the great problems of power in the political sphere—the use of physical force, and the relationship of authority's power to individual liberty. If the conclusions reached seem consistently akin to those generally espoused by men of good will, that fact is not an argument for the superfluity of natural law but for its necessity in rationally justifying desirable values which good will alone cannot justify or sustain.

PART II

The Ordering of Power

V

Natural Law for the Twentieth Century

THE DISCUSSION of natural law in this chapter is not something spun out of the writer's head; both conceptual bases and terminology have been refined through literally thousands of years of thought and usage. But much misconception has likewise accumulated, and it must be removed before those seeking a moral foundation for politics can recognize the necessity for a conscious return to something the repudiation of which has never actually been required by either logic or new knowledge.

At the outset, we may go so far as to say that no system of political ethics which *demands* the obedience of men on the basis of moral obligation can have validity unless it involves certain concepts which, taken together, equal the natural law, no matter how reluctant men are to use that designation. This will seem like a large and, to many, a preposterous claim for what it is still fashionable to consider an outmoded medieval theory. Even when properly understood such theory may well continue to be unacceptable to those who insist on clinging to anachronistic nineteenth century superstitions and shibboleths. But in this century of the breaking of nations, sincere men must reexamine their assumptions and at least give serious thought to an approach which not only has had the advocacy of many great thinkers since Plato and Aristotle, but is implicit in those concepts of political morality espoused by men of good will today.

The very mention of the term natural law has often been sufficient to bring forth polemical abuse, and examples of harsh criticism are not difficult to find. There is Jeremy Bentham's famous attempt at a *coup de grâce:* "A great multitude of people are continually talking of the Law of Nature; and then they go on giving you their sentiments about what is right and wrong; and these sentiments, you are to understand, are so many chapters and sections of the Law of Nature." [1] To Hegel the law of nature was nothing but a "fraud which is inseparably involved in the method of the understanding and its arguings, namely, giving a good reason for a bad thing and assuming that in that way one has justified it"; [2] while Thomas Cooper demanded with sarcastic curiosity: "Theoretical writers like Grotius, Pufendorf, Barbeyrac, Heineccius, Vattel, Rutherford, Burlamaqui and others, boast of a law of nature or of nations existing. When was it enacted? By whom? or by what power has it been sanctioned." [3] More recent writers like Sir Thomas Holland and William Graham Sumner dismiss it lightly as "of the nature of a legal fiction," [4] or as simply rationalized expression of the folkways.[5] And so on *ad infinitum.*[6]

---

[1] *Introduction to the Principles of Morals and Legislation*, Oxford, 1892, from the new ed. of 1823, p. 18, note 6.
[2] *Philosophy of Right*, trans. S. W. Dyde, London, 1896, p. 29.
[3] *Lectures on the Principles of Political Economy*, London, 1826, pp. 53–54.
[4] *Lectures on International Law*, 10th ed., London, 1933, p. 18.
[5] *Selected Essays*, ed. A. G. Keller and M. R. Davie, New Haven, 1924, pp. 9–11.
[6] For other contributions to the negative crescendo, see John Austin, *Lectures on Jurisprudence*, 5th ed., London, 1911, II, 88; John W. Burgess, *Political Science and Comparative Constitutional Law*, New York, 1891, p. 289; James Q. Dealey, *The State and Government*, New York, 1921, p. 278; Frank J. Goodnow, *Social Reform and the Constitution*, New York, 1911, p. 3; Jeremiah Jenks, *Principles of Politics*, New York, 1909, p. 23; A. Lawrence Lowell, *Essays on Government*, Boston, 1889, p. 193; George L. Scherger, *The Evolution of Modern Liberty*, New York, 1904, p. 11; W. F. Willoughby, *Introduction to the Government of Modern*

These verbal flagellations indicate a profound aversion to whatever its critics suppose the natural law to be, but many rail and carp and scoff at a straw man, with the amount of sneer often directly proportional to the degree of distortion. Ask for a definition, and the modern anti-naturalist is likely to give a good description of one of the things which the traditional natural law is definitely not.

To begin with, it has nothing to do with the hypothetical conduct of man in a primitive and uncontaminated state of nature. Fanciful seventeenth century anthropology, with its vision of savages gamboling *in puris naturalibus,* led to fanciful ethical and legal theory which assumed that the most humane and virtuous of men's acts and opinions were carry-overs from the golden age before tailors.[7] It was scarcely any wonder that nineteenth-century writers could find little but ridicule for

---

States, New York, 1919, pp. 166–168; W. W. Willoughby, *An Examination of the Nature of the State,* New York, 1896, p. 115; also his *Ethical Basis of Political Authority,* New York, 1930, p. 244.

For a good example of the same sort of thing in a court decision, see *North American Dredging Company of Texas v. United Mexican States* (1926), reprinted *in toto,* in *American Journal of International Law,* XX (1926), 800 (see especially p. 804). And for a classic off-the-record statement by Judge Gary floundering in an attempt at philosophy, see the quotation from his speech made early in 1925 at the Waldorf, New York, in *America,* XXXII (1925), 501.

[7] Leading exponents of the new naturalism were Pufendorf with his *De jure naturae et gentium,* reproduction of the edition of 1688, trans. C. H. and W. A. Oldfather, Oxford, 1934; Thomasius, *Fundamenta juris naturae et gentium,* 1705; Burlamaqui, *Principes du droit naturel et politique,* 1747; Rutherford, *Institutes of Natural Law,* 1754; and Vattel, *Le droit des gens,* reproduction of edition of 1758, trans. Charles G. Fenwick, Washington, 1916. Though usually classified as a member of the so-called Eclectic School, Vattel took over the state of nature theory without reservations.

Sir Henry Maine also accuses Grotius of subscribing to such a standard of primitivism, but with scant justice. The great Dutch jurist was much closer to the scholastic tradition than Sir Henry realized; in fact it never seems to have occurred to the nineteenth century legal historian that such a tradition existed. See his *International Law* (Whewell Lectures, 1887), London, 1888, p. 22.

such a chimerical norm of conduct, especially when early field research indicated that modern primitives had often come just as far from the first Utopia as their more civilized brethren. Unfortunately, this "primitivist" basis for standards had gradually become identified with the natural law as such; and mere nominal relationship often proved a source of initial anathema for every concept of natural law. Significantly enough, that school of international law theory which stems from Pufendorf is popularly called the Pure Law of Nature School. Only a few modern commentators have as yet grasped the basic anomaly of such a label.[8]

Attempts at refinement of the crude "state of nature" theory had, of course, been made during the eighteenth century. More sophisticated political thinkers, like the American founding fathers, reasoned in

terms of a philosophical preconception rather than an historical state or condition. In other words, the laws of nature or the rights derived from nature's laws were those which exist or which man has, not because of any human legislation, but because they are inseparable from the nature of things and the constitution of man. Such theories ordinarily are to the effect that in a civil condition there are certain rights which may not be exercised, and which are therefore not "natural" to it, but that if the restraints of political organization were removed, as, for example, in the case of a revolution, those rights would revert to individuals.[9]

Apart from embodying the age-old fallacy of man against the state and the implication that man at his best is a nonpolitical animal, such an approach was bound to end in sterility, though for a time, during the American and French revolutionary period, it played its role in a dynamic movement. The phi-

[8] One of these few is Professor J. L. Brierley. See his *The Law of Nations*, Oxford, 1928, p. 28.
[9] Benjamin F. Wright, Jr., *American Interpretations of Natural Law*, Cambridge, Mass., 1931, pp. 337–338.

losophy of the Enlightenment was actually pretty much of a hodgepodge, superficially sparkling and ultrarational, but never thought through to its final implications and the discarding of incompatible premises. To Jefferson, for example, the "state of nature" concept was never really a logically necessary part of his political theory, though in the abstract sense described above, he probably thought it was. The creative aspect of eighteenth century revolutionary theory was the doctrine of natural rights, stemming from the far older and more viable scholastic tradition; [10] but its effect was counteracted before the turn of the century by the non-progressive tendencies inherent in the "state of nature" approach. When *the* right is linked to a past state—even if only conceptually—rather than to present conditions, rights and duties inevitably freeze into a static system, which in turn can easily be identified with the system of rights and duties then prevailing and thus used as a hard-shell defense of the *status quo*. Hence the persistently reactionary application of the so-called Higher Law in American constitutional history, the court-nurtured growth of the legal concept of vested rights which, by shielding privilege and property under the cloak of "nature," did so much to discredit nature's law with men of progressive and liberal mind.[11] From the exalted role of rationale for advancing justice, the natural law had fallen to be nothing more than a smug apology for economic exploitation.[12]

[10] For a scholarly study of the connection between eighteenth century American democratic ideals and the scholastic tradition, see John A. Ryan and Moorhouse F. X. Millar, S.J., *The State and the Church*, New York, 1922, Chaps. V–VII. See also Gaillard Hunt, "The Virginia Declaration of Rights and Cardinal Bellarmine," *Catholic Historical Review*, III (1917), 276.

[11] See Edward S. Corwin, "The Basic Doctrine of American Constitutional Law," *Michigan Law Review*, XII (1914), 247; also his "Higher Law Background of American Constitutional Law," *Harvard Law Review*, XLII (1928), 149, (1929), 365 for an excellent account of this development.

[12] See such famous Supreme Court cases as *Allgeyer v. Louisiana* (1897),

A simultaneous development which further obscured the traditional meaning of natural law was the gradual mechanization of the concept. The surge of interest in physical nature as the object of all-conquering science, the secularization of ethics, politics and law, swept aside old distinctions and established categories of thought; and the natural law of science began to absorb the traditional juristic-ethical law of nature. The process took several hundred years, but already in the eighteenth century the French Encyclopedists attempted to make natural law nothing more than conclusions from observation of physical nature expressed in quantitative terms. From being defined as the "ultimate principle of fitness with regard to the nature of man considered as a rational or a social being," the natural law eventually came to be regarded as applying to all creatures, reasonable or unreasonable, animate or inanimate, as the principle of physical necessity in their conduct or activity.[13] The stars in their courses and men in their deeds were held slaves of the same mathematical formulae—a concept to which the more developed determinism of the nineteenth century, with its human puppets whirling between the twin poles of heredity and environment, provided a fitting annotation. Such an attempt to equate rules of conduct with invariable physical law could lead only to unnatural compression and further sterility. The analogy of physical necessity seeped into all fields of social thought, forcing out voluntaristic morality and bearing early fruit in such a distortion as Buckle's geographical

165 U.S. 578; *Lochner v. New York* (1905), 198 U.S. 45, wherein the natural law, partially disguised as rights guarded by the Constitution, was used judicially to crush economic reform legislation.

[13] This gradual change, beginning in the sixteenth century, is well traced by Sir Frederick Pollock in "The History of the Law of Nature," *Columbia Law Review*, I (1901), 11. Perhaps the first inklings are in St. Germain's noted *Doctor and Student*, though he still makes a distinction between what he calls the law of nature specially and generally considered.

determinism. If many determinists could not stomach the crudely amoral implications of their faith and continued to work for reform on moral grounds, they nevertheless maintained their belief in this "scientific" law of nature, expressed in terms of whatever new theory such shamans as Haeckel, Freud, Watson, *et al.*, could conjure up for members of the creed. That capacity for cultivating logical blind spots which has marked so many liberals was utilized to the utmost.

Nazi theorists managed to concoct an even more unique version of natural law, further to muddle the term's meaning. To them it was a law imbedded in the perception of the *Volk* (people),[14]—something peculiar to each people or nation, not absolute but relative, atune to the continually changing needs of a *Volk* as determined by its rights of existence. "*Naturrecht ist Lebensrecht.*"[15] There is, of course, nothing wrong with the law's keeping abreast of changing needs; in fact in the long run any legal system must do so or perish. But when the right of a *Volk* becomes the sole source of rights, regardless of other peoples and individuals with whom it must have relations, then the law which purports to justify such a right is nothing but a poor mask for sheer national selfishness. Moreover, by making law rise from the mysterious depths of *Blut und Boden* (blood and soil) in which it finds origin and nurture, this Nazi theory completely repudiated the use of reason as mode of cognition, in fact denied the ultimate rationality of the very principles of law themselves.

HUMAN NATURE, THE NORM OF ACTION

Some 2,000 years ago Horace wrote in his *Ars Poetica*, "Naturam furca expellas, tamen usque recurret" (You may

---

[14] H. H. Dietze, *Naturrecht in der Gegenwart*, Bonn, 1936, p. 39.
[15] See R. Eberhard, *Modernes Naturrecht ein rechtsphilosophischer Versuch*, Rostock, 1934, p. 40.

drive out nature with a pitchfork, but she will come back every time). The Roman poet's aphorism expressed at least part of a great truth. Many thinkers among the ancients similarly held that there is a natural way of doing things, that men can act unnaturally if they so desire, but that inexorably nature catches up with them. And so they logically concluded that the natural way is the rational way, which is something altogether different from saying, as Hegel later did, that the real is the rational; [16] for the real, the existent situation at any given time, is not always the natural.

The question of whether nature always catches up with those who defy her is an important one and the answer less obvious than it seemed to the Greeks and Romans. Unlike Horace, the scholastics made no claim that she does come back every time she is chased out with a pitchfork, though they are willing to give her credit for fair regularity. In fact the relative need for her coming back every time furnished one of the major distinctions between ancient and medieval natural law theory. We do not mean that these versions were antithetical, or entirely on different levels; for the later adopted what was valid in the earlier and built upon it. Today, neo-scholastics likewise admit that the arguments of Aristotle, Plato, and the Stoics are convincing up to a point, and will even use them to make that point. They are very likely to begin answering modern critics of the natural law in much the same way as Cicero answered its ancient critics.

While the natural law is not to be confused with the mathematically expressed laws of physical science, this does not mean it has nothing to do with physical nature. For the law of nature concerns itself with the *nature* or essence of man, and with all

---

[16] This, of course, is the implication of Hegel's idealistic philosophy of development. See his *Logic*, trans. William Wallace, Oxford, 1892, pp. 1 ff.

other natures or essences which, in their concrete embodiments, are related to the thought and activity of man. The element of rational interpretation and evaluation must, however, always dominate, for physical nature has many laws which alone provide no criterion of moral judgment. It is perfectly *natural* to throw a rock; it is perfectly *natural* for the rock to gain momentum and smash any skull which gets in its way; it is perfectly *natural* for the person with smashed skull to fall down and die. Every vicious deed, every cruel blow, is perfectly *natural* once the doer sets those forces in action which normally lead to such a result. That is why wariness is so necessary when people prate of the natural man, free from all sordid inhibitions, who must be allowed to follow every impulse of his nature because to do what he wants to do and can do is only natural. To some this sort of argument may seem as dated as the Freudian craze, bathtub gin, and Greenwich Village Bohemianism which nurtured it. The stern hard realities of our century's fourth and fifth decades have shown that man contains darker springs of action, more hideous potencies of cruelty, than can safely be left uninhibited. But flamboyant naturalism is a persistently recurring aberration, and its practice continues widely in this era of discarded standards and moral breakdown.

Discriminating between various actions which are physically natural, natural law theory is something far more subtle than an excuse for libertinism. It is essentially a philosophic ethic, grounded in hard reality. It provides the means for rational evaluation of things as they are in terms of things as they ought to be, covering the area of free human relations with the external world. The natural law is a moral law the subjects of which are physically, though not morally, free to violate it in defiance of the sanction which such breach invokes. The Germans would call it a *Soll-Gesetz* as distinguished from a

Muss-Gesetz. It thus frankly implies a voluntaristic psychology, and even great Stoics like Seneca and Cicero were forced to discard the theoretical determinism of their metaphysics when discussing natural law and ethics.

Most people think they know what law means, but the word is slippery. One person will define it in terms of the lawgiver, another in terms of those subject to it, a third in terms of its purpose; but all seem to agree that, somehow or other, law implies a norm of action, expresses a certain regularity of conduct under the same conditions, either demanded in the case of free moral beings or imposed and necessarily conformed to in the case of unfree beings.

If law, then, involves a norm of conduct, and the natural law involves a norm of conduct for free and rational men, where is that norm to be found? Precisely where the ancients and medieval scholastics found it. Not in fiery precepts writ across the face of a cloud, not in the solemn decrees of high tribunals, but simply in human nature itself, not a stunted or a partial nature, or some particular aspect of it, but the fullness of the human complex with its many relationships to being: "all man's faculties, all his essential relations, and all these arranged in their proper hierarchy." [17] Functionalism saturates the natural law ethic, and that which is right is that which is suitable to the nature of the thing acting or acted upon, in harmony with the inherent ordination of means and ends deriving from the essence of a being which will help to evolve the perfections of that essence.[18] The ethical universe is therefore both a rational and a

[17] Stephen J. Rueve, "The Philosophy of the Natural Moral Law," *The Modern Schoolman*, XIV (1937), 31.

[18] St. Thomas Aquinas has a very pertinent paragraph on the essence of man's essence: "It must be observed that the nature of a thing is chiefly the form from which that thing derives its species. Now man derives his species from his rational soul: and consequently whatever is contrary to the order of reason is, properly speaking, contrary to the nature of man, as

hierarchical universe in which one can tell precious from less precious, significant from insignificant, in which proper order requires subordination of lower to higher values, both within and without the human creature.

Purposeless activity means irrational activity. In a rational order, essences determine the functional and hence the moral desirability of ends towards which activity may be directed. Natural law theory therefore implies the existence of a constant factor in human nature, and is incompatible with any Heraclitean philosophy of perpetual and all-embracing flux. If, of course, there is no such thing as a distinctive human essence, if man amounts to nothing more than a "fortuitous collocation of atoms," then to speak of human nature as a norm is absurd. The individual person can have no value, and therefore, as we have already seen, no valid argument remains for the ethical control of conduct. Psychological anarchism can lead only to social and political anarchism, and the denial of personality opens the door to unrestricted bestiality.

THE MODE OF COGNITION

If human nature is the general standard of natural law, how can this norm be applied in concrete cases? In other words, what is the specific mode of its cognition? Clear concepts and precise language will avoid much confusion on this point, for our method of knowing is intimately bound up with our notion of what we know. As a matter of fact, many definitions of natural law are actually in terms of the way we cognize it, or at least

---

man; while whatever is in accord with reason, is in accord with the nature of man, as man. *Now man's good is to be in accord with reason, and his evil is to be against reason*, as Dionysius states, (Div. Nom. iv). Therefore human virtue, which makes a man good, and his works good, is in accord with man's nature, for as much as it accords with his reason: while vice is contrary to man's nature, in so far as it is contrary to the order of reason." *Summa Theologica*, I–II, 71, 2c.

imply a mode of cognition without saying very much about the norm of conduct itself.

Appeal is often made to "that law graven in the heart of man"; and with qualification of several terms—of *heart* to symbolize human nature rather than seat of the emotions, of *graven* to mean inherent in rather than impressed upon—the metaphor may shakily pass muster as a partial statement. But some people have a congenital horror of ambiguous, poetically suggestive definitions—and the word heart bears with it all sorts of emotional connotations. It brings to mind that "small inner voice" of unknown larynx which whispers to the Illuminati, the sensitively perceptive. And as soon as conduct becomes a matter of private revelation and emotional response, uniformity goes out the window, and with it usually morality.

Right and wrong do not hinge on what Arnold Lunn has called "fif"—a positive or negative *feeling* about something rising from the bones. Yet while the correlation of morality with emotion may seem like an elementary error, many influential ethical philosophers have begun by muddling the process of knowing good and evil, and logically have ended with degree of spine-tingle as their highest criterion. Thinkers like Shaftesbury,[19] Hutcheson,[20] and Kant,[21] though differing of course in the working out of theory, agreed in assuming a special faculty by which humans distinguish proper from improper conduct—the so-called moral sense. But if we do not arrive at ethical judgments by reason, then we must arrive at them without reason, irrationally; and so to Hume the moral sense became merely a sentiment, "an immediate feeling and finer internal

---

[19] See his *Characteristics of Men, Manners, Opinions, Times,* 3 vols., London, 1711.
[20] See his *A System of Moral Philosophy,* 2 vols., London, 1755.
[21] See his *Kritik des Praktischen Vernunft,* Vol. V in *Saemtliche Werke,* Leipzig, 1867–1868.

sense" which operates wholly apart from the intellect.[22] James Martineau then climaxed the process in writing: "A state of sentiency, be its seat or be its cause what it may—an emotion, a relish, a disgust—is something of which I am recipient in virtue of a passive susceptibility; it knows nothing; it does nothing; it is simply felt." [23]

We do not wish to disparage the emotional reaction which may take place after the recognition of good or evil. Without indignation, horror, joy, grief, and other emotions abetting morality, the path of virtue might well be too arid for the generality of men. Nor is there any point in denying that every-day moral judgments for most people do not involve analysis but derive largely from accepted modes of conduct handed down from generation to generation or absorbed from the milieu. However, such everyday moral judgments must, in the last analysis, be consistent with a rational appraisal of reality if they are to survive, and certainly provide no argument for making an irrational factor the ultimate basis of ethical cognition. Instead they point to the necessity for sound principles on the part of those leaders of men who influence popular standards and conduct.

A more subtle confusion, found among some scholastics and constituting a fine example of how mere repetition of a formula can lull the critical faculties, has stemmed from St. Thomas Aquinas' famous definition of natural law as the "participation of the eternal law in the rational creature." [24] Obviously a key word here is "participation," and for once St. Thomas' choice does not seem as happy as it might have been. In a certain sense

[22] Cited and commented on by Timothy Brosnahan, "Ethics: a Science," *The Modern Schoolman*, XIII (1936), 77.
[23] *Types of Ethical Theory*, Oxford, 1891, II, 476.
[24] "Participatio legis aeternae in rationali creatura." *Summa Theologica*, I–II, 91, 2c.

natural law is the participation of the eternal law in the rational creature, but not in a clear sense demanding no qualification.

Some scholastics identify this "participation" with a natural, innate inclination toward the acts proper to man, a kind of shining on man of the divine light by which he can tell good from evil.[25] In other words, the natural law "comes natural" like breathing and sleeping. There appears to be no essential distinction between such a view and making conscience a separate faculty, operating by itself to sense or feel or know good and evil. "Innate inclination" in the concrete can mean nothing but having a capacity for ethical intuition, or for some other form of non-rational cognition.

Most scholastics, however, shy away from anything smacking of illuminism or innatism, be the latter Platonic or Cartesian. While the well-known medieval epistemological maxim, "Nihil in intellectu quod non prius in sensu" (Nothing is in the mind which was not first in the sense), has been criticized for failing to take into account the direct apprehension of form,[26] it remains true that the moral judgment in the concrete case, like all other specific judgments, must be based on intellectual knowledge which, in turn, normally and ultimately must derive from sense knowledge.

If "participation" is taken to mean merely that the natural capacity and impulse of the intellect is to strive for truth, that correct moral judgments are a part of the great universe of truth which the intellect is adapted to discover, that the natural moral law is part of the eternal moral law, and that by having

[25] See for example: Victor Cathrein, *Moralphilosophie*, 2 vols., Freiburg, 1904, I, 380; Thomas Slater, *A Manual of Moral Philosophy*, 3d ed., New York, 1908, I, 116; Cardinal Tommaso Maria Zigliara, *Ethics*, in Vol. III of *Summa Philosophica*, 10th ed., Paris, 1895, 24, I.
[26] See for example E. I. Watkin, *A Philosophy of Form*, New York, 1935, pp. 86 ff.

such capacity to discover the natural law as part of the eternal law the rational creature in a sense therefore "participates" passively and potentially in the eternal law, then the word may pass muster. Or, viewing the matter ontologically rather than psychologically, one can say that the natural law is the participation of the eternal law in the rational creature inasmuch as the natural law is that part of the eternal moral law which applies to the rational creature and, in fact, takes its principles from his essence and function.

But no matter what the word be understood to signify, such elasticity of meaning does not make for clarity and precision. Little is gained by continuing to use "participation" in discussing the natural law. St. Thomas would have been the last person in the world to insist that every definition of his be retained uncritically just because he had proposed it.

Even though it contains not a hint of innatism or ethical intuitionism, no definition of natural law purely in terms of mode of cognition will be adequate. Three important factors require consideration: (1) the way things are, which provides the norm of conduct and is the basis in reality of the rule; (2) the way in which we cognize this reality; and (3) the way we express in words and propositions, in order to make a rule, the precepts discovered in the way things are. Now of these the natural law is not the way we cognize but what we cognize, just as it is not the mere verbal expression of that cognition, though including it, for verbal expression in the form of a proposition is essential if the intellect of man is to grasp a rule of action. Tentatively then, we may define the natural law as a moral norm of action which reason discovers by examination of the functional order that exists objectively in the nature of man and his relation to other men and to the external world. For the time being, this will serve as a framework for discussion, though as a definition it will probably seem a bit too simple in the light of our continuing analysis.

To many the picture of hard, cold, abstractive reason digging into the turmoil of life to separate right from wrong demands an explanation. The scholastics have an old maxim: "Whatever is received is received according to the nature of the recipient." Thus man receives knowledge according to the nature of his knowing faculties, which, upon attainment of maturity and apart from admitted individual defect or possibility of error, are conceived to be intrinsically capable of arriving at objective truth with complete certitude. That is the epistemological assumption of natural law theory, and without it there can be only intellectual and moral shambles.[27] Professor Max Huber's rather naive attempt to compare the natural law with a scientist's working hypothesis is nothing but Vaihinger's "as if" philosophy all over again without benefit of the latter's more subtle argumentation.[28] If it is to influence conduct, a system of morality needs grounding on something more firm than an assumption which further experimentation may admittedly show to be ill-founded.

Now the conclusions of deductive reason are, in the last analysis, the conclusions of a syllogism, express or implied.[29] But from where do the major and minor premises of conclusions about the natural law come? They are not simply pulled out of a hat. They are based on reality, on the perennial facts of human existence. Just as certain self-evident principles of reason exist in the speculative order, so in the moral order there are principles evident to anyone that comprehends the

[27] See above, pp. 59 ff.
[28] See Max Huber, *Die soziologischen Grundlagen des Voelkerrechts,* 2d ed., Berlin, 1928, pp. 34-35.
[29] See Thomas Crumley, C.S.C., *Logic: Deductive and Inductive,* New York, 1934, pp. 181 ff.

meaning of their component terms,[30] and these are "known by the intellect to possess a necessary and universal validity which is not due to the constitution of the mind, but is inherent in the objective reality" of being.[31]

Self-evident obviously does not mean self-evident at birth, or necessarily at any time during life to all men. Comprehension of component terms demands not only the ability to comprehend but also the devotion of some thought to their analysis, for it is absurd to expect a meaning to be self-evidently true to a person who does not know what the meaning means. Self-evident truths do not pop into the mind uninvited out of thin air; but when their significance is grasped, the unescapable necessity of their truth seizes the mind.

Thus if we admit the existence of a moral order and know what good and evil mean, it is self-evident that we *ought* to do good and avoid evil—and this is a primary principle of natural law.[32] If, of course, we deny that a moral order exists, the principle no longer has any validity; but there is no known ethical code (and anthropologists are not likely to find one) based on the principle: Do evil and avoid good. Notions of what specifically constitutes good and evil may sometimes vary, but not the general attitude of people as to what their relationship to those terms *ought* to be in all cases.

Likewise if we admit the existence of a functional order, a universe of being impregnated with final causation in which each creature has its appointed end, it is a self-evident prin-

---

[30] As St. Thomas has put it: "The primary precepts of the law of nature stand to the practical reason as the first principles of scientific demonstration do to the speculative reason: for both sets of principles are self-evident." *Summa Theologica*, I–II, 94, 2.

[31] Timothy Brosnahan, *op. cit.*, p. 80.

[32] "Bonum est faciendum et prosequendum, et malum vitandum." *Summa Theologica*, I–II, 94, 2.

ciple that doing good is conforming to our natures in all essential aspects, and hence achieving our end; that doing evil is not conforming to our natures, and not achieving our end. As we have indicated, this functionalism permeates the entire tissue of natural law morality; it applies not only to man in the abstract, but to each part of man in the concrete, and to each part of the non-human universe subordinate to man which fulfills its function in helping man to fulfill his function.

The cognition of proper function involves both observation and reasoning. We obtain help from the study of theodicy, ontology, cosmology, and psychology. We use the inductive as well as deductive method, for we learn the natural way of things by observing nature. And facts thus observed provide subject matter for the specific principles of natural law which fit into the larger framework of the great primary principles. The actual moral precepts then take shape as "the progressive application of a first principle by obvious or increasingly complex reasoning to classes of action more and more particular"; and "every dictate of reason, commanding or forbidding an individual action, is a conclusion of reason founded ultimately on a first principle" [33] but drawing its relevance from hard concrete reality.

The traditional scholastic view of conscience makes it, in fact, not a faculty, a habit, or some mysterious "still small voice whispering to the soul," but an act, a practical judgment, of the understanding, forbidding, allowing, or commanding an action. "It is virtually the conclusion of a syllogism, the major premise of which would be some general principle of command or counsel in moral matters; the minor, a statement of fact bringing some particular case of your own conduct under that law; and the conclusion, which is conscience, a decision of

[33] Timothy Brosnahan, *op. cit.*

the case for yourself according to that principle." [34] Conscience is thus, to a certain extent, simply the process of cognizing and applying natural law; and the expression, "natural law of conscience," seems especially apt.[35] The syllogistic mode of reasoning need not, of course, be used before each ethical decision. A great body of moral truth, over which members of society have virtually habitual hold because of the traditions and mores of that society, comes to individuals by a process called synteresis; and numerous simple actions are performed or refrained from on moral grounds without analysis.

Natural law precepts may be either easy or difficult to arrive at. Reason seizes upon self-evident *primary* principles, and from these, other dictates of reason, or *secondary* principles, logically and directly flow. These latter raise few issues of interpretation or phrasing. Applying to many general cases, they are clear, quickly and indubitably. But there are also *tertiary* precepts which, applying to few and specialized cases, demand investigation, taking shape only after a long and involved process of inference. Before becoming part of the mores of a culture, they may be preached only by wise men crying in the wilderness; and it is these tenuous, often disputed, extensions of natural law to the periphery of the logical universe, beyond which the pure reason cannot wander without wavering and losing certitude, that require supplementation by positive law, human and divine.[36]

Natural law precepts may either command the doing of something or allow it to be done at option, as well as forbid an action, though the negative concept of law as a ban on conduct overshadows its affirmative function in the minds of most peo-

[34] Joseph Rickaby, S.J., *Moral Philosophy*, London, 1918, p. 135.
[35] Conscience is, of course, the cognition and application not only of natural law precepts, but also of positive moral law.
[36] See Albert Valensin, *Traité de droit naturel*, 2 vols., Paris, 1921, I, 197.

ple, especially those with a diluted Calvinist background. Since any injunction to action may be expressed as a prohibition against not so acting, this tendency to think of law as being "agin something" often shows itself in inverted popular phrasing. Thus the pupil thinks in terms of a school regulation against his coming late to classes even when the rule expressly states that he must come to his classes on time. The distinction may seem hypercritical, but it does not make for a clear grasp of the reason behind a functional moral order to state a positive rule in terms of something which ought not to be.

OBLIGATION AND SANCTION

The question of individual obligation to the natural law is closely linked to the question of the natural law's source. Throughout the ages, thinkers have followed one of two paths of approach which apparently run in opposite directions yet ultimately meet. To Aristotle, Plato, Cicero, Seneca, and most of the ancients, the abstract idea of virtue creates the obligation of natural law.[37] Moral excellence becomes an end in itself, and moral excellence consists in the fulfillment of function according to one's specific nature.[38] In technical jargon, such an approach is aretaic rather than deontological,[39] shifting the emphasis from duty towards an extrinsic source of law to obligation towards the individual personality or subject of law itself.[40]

[37] See Plato, *Republic*, IV, 443, and 444d; *Laws*, IV, 716c; Aristotle, *Nicomachean Ethics*, II, 1107a; III, 1110a 26 *sqq*.; Cicero, *De finibus*, III, 5; *Diogenes Laertes*, VII, 88.

[38] To Aristotle such fulfillment achieves a mean, to Plato a harmony. See *Nicom. Eth.*, II, 6, 1106b 36; *Republic*, IV, 443.

[39] A dramatist like Aeschylus was much less secularistic in his concept of natural law than the philosophers. See the famous passage in *Antigone*, verses 446 to 480.

[40] Professor Rueve puts it concisely: "In Plato's writings there is seldom any clear proposition—and never any development—to the effect that

That may seem rather a tenuous basis for a categorical imperative—and so it is. But the ancients thought they had another compelling reason for obedience. While they did not grasp the need for true moral obligation, neither did they put all their trust in mere intellectual satisfaction resulting from realization of personal compatibility with a rational functional order. For "drive out nature with a pitchfork and she will come back every time." The poet might well have added, "and she will come back with a pitchfork." The ancients believed that if man lives irrationally, that is, unnaturally, nature will provide its own sanction in accordance with a great and universal law of retribution. Perversion of function tends to destroy the ability to function at all; action contrary to nature is itself ultimately contrary to action. Virtue is its own reward,[41] for without virtue there can be no good life. The unnatural man is the unhappy man, and only the man who lives rationally, according to nature, enjoys "eudaimonia" or happiness, which Aristotle identifies with the highest good.[42]

Now no one will deny that abused nature can kick back like a Missouri mule. Any toper with a bad hangover will vouch for that. Our whole contemporary world is full of glaring examples of perverted function working havoc to individuals and nations; but there remains a logical flaw in this secularistic natural law, though it sounds like an ironclad argument to say that essences determine ends, that the end of man is happiness,

---

. . . obligation comes from the Legislator of the universe. And (so far as I am aware) the notion of divine legislator is entirely foreign to Aristotle." *Op. cit.*, p. 31.

[41] The maxim is actually more characteristically Stoic than Aristotelian or Platonic. See Cicero, *Diogenes Laertes*, VII, 102; Seneca, *Ep.* 85.

[42] "As far as the name goes, there is quite general agreement; for both the vulgar multitude and the refined say that it is eudaimonia and furthermore they conceive 'living well' and 'doing well' as synonomous with 'being happy.'" *Nicomachean Ethics*, I, 1095a 17.

that the fulfillment of essential function is the means to happiness, and that one can therefore erect a valid ethical system on the basis of pure functionalism. It falls apart in the fact of great catastrophe sweeping away both innocent and guilty, in the face of the swindling but unjailed millionaire, the grafting but reelected politician, the ruthless dictator rising to power on the blood of his victims—all of whom may be as "happy" at any given time as the "good" man. In other words, a secular natural law must assume the inevitability of mundane retribution to claim obedience, and that is precisely what its advocates cannot guarantee. The mere possibility of retribution is often not enough to deter the clever from action, but may simply put a premium on their cleverness, on taking all necessary precautions. Then too, the Louis XV's of this world are not likely to reform even when they know that the heads of the Louis XVI's will roll. If only "aprés moi le deluge," why bother about the present? Erring and transgressing mortals are only too willing to pass consequences on to those who follow.

Few will deny that so-called "pangs of conscience" can sometimes spoil the enjoyment of wrongdoing and its fruits, but sensitivity of emotional reaction is often inversely proportional to the burden which conscience must bear. Morality needs to rest on something more objective than possible mental hauntings, which may not exist, or in any case may be insignificant compared to the satisfaction derived from the commission of wrong.

Peripatetics still dispute the exact meaning of "eudaimonia"; but it makes little difference here whether the term is precisely translatable as happiness or bears more subtle connotations; whether happiness means merely what John Cowper Powys has called that "particular glow of well-being that arises when something deep in us is being satisfied and fulfilled," [43] or some-

[43] *The Art of Happiness*, New York, 1935, p. 5.

thing as basic as "an operation of the soul in the way of excellence, in a complete life." [44] The essential point remains that Aristotle could not cite universal experience in answering the person who claims: "My concept of 'eudaimonia' works pretty well for me and I am satisfied with it, though it has very little to do with leading the good life which you advocate."

Though Aristotle and others of the ancients would have been horrified at the thought, their secular natural law leads logically to sheer utilitarianism which, as we have seen, fails completely as criterion of morality. Good always pays, they argued, but they could never convince the man who proves by his conduct that evil pays. The same general criticism applies to a modern attempt like that of Professor George Catlin to resurrect a secular law of nature. "That which is contrary to Natural Law cannot be historically successful," he claims; [45] but whatever test of historical success is assumed, it is not likely that the mere possibility of long-term retribution to future generations will deter many in the short run. A utilitarian code which has nothing more to offer than a vague verdict of history at which few historians have been able to arrive will make fewer converts among the amoral seekers of power in our time.

In his approach to the problem, the modern scholastic does not begin from scratch. He admits that the ancients had a good though overworked point, but realizes that another point needs making, which cannot be made so long as the argument stays purely on a secular plane. He reemphasizes that human nature is the norm of morality, but to this there is added the act of a higher Legislator speaking through the medium of the natural law. Moral obligation takes on new meaning, and right becomes more than a functional necessity, wrong more than a monkey

[44] *Nicomachean Ethics*, I, 1097b 1.
[45] *The Story of the Political Philosophers*, New York, 1939, p. 761.

wrench in the system. The natural law is also the divine law, and violations of it are not only against nature but against nature's God. Thus to add to the sanctions which an outraged nature and society may inflict on violators, there is also the sanction implicit in a universal moral order for those who disturb that order.

The scholastic, then, lists three types of sanction for the law of nature: (1) those rising from the individual order, which include remorse of conscience, disease of body and mind, and slavery to vicious habits; (2) those rising from the social order, which include loss of security, friendship, and love; and finally (3) that rising from the universal order, which is the danger of losing one's last end by willfully turning away from that end in breaching the natural law.[46]

PROPERTIES AND SPECIFICATIONS

The properties of a thing derive directly from its essence, and it is convenient to discuss further aspects of the natural law under the headings of what are usually called its four properties: unity, clarity, universality, and immutability. By *unity* is meant the singleness of source, end, and logical construction which characterizes the natural law. Its Author is one, its purpose for all men is the same, and as part of the great universe of being, it is subject to the great metaphysical principle of unity. Finally, in the order of evidence, it achieves the unity of deductive derivation from the never-changing ultimate principle: Do good and avoid evil.

By *clarity* is meant that the natural law is knowable to the generality of men—at least in its primary and secondary precepts. No person with developed reason can plead invincible

[46] See Ignatius W. Cox, *Liberty, Its Use and Abuse*, New York, 1939, pp. 74 ff.; J. Eliot Ross, *Ethics*, New York, 1938, p. 92; or any other scholastic treatise on ethics.

ignorance as excuse for not observing these basic principles, though of course bad logic, perverted will, uncontrolled passion, and evil habit can smother moral truth. Most of the confusion and ignorance about natural law really involves tertiary precepts or complicated applications of principle in specialized cases. Professor Gilson has stated the position so well that we can do no better than repeat his words:

One may . . . ask how it is that usages and customs are so different in different countries, and how it is that men with the same human nature draw from the same principles of the natural law conclusions that are so basically different. It is because of the difference between the sciences and the speculative reason, which relate to law as universal and necessary, and the moral and practical reason which relate to law as particular and contingent. The principles of the natural law are the same in all countries and among all peoples, and the most general deductions from them are usually the same among all. But the farther we come down towards more and more specific prescriptions, the more the chances of error in the deduction increase; interest and sentiment enter in, evil dispositions interfere with thought, so much so that, though a man sets out reasoning from principles of natural law, he comes to will acts that contradict it. This is why the natural law, which is one for all men, seems manifold and discordant among different individuals. It is unchangeable in itself, and its principles cannot be torn from the heart of man, but it appears variable and is sometimes obfuscated by error in its application to details.[47]

But with all this fine reasoning about the causes of error, this distinction between different kinds of precepts, the suspicion may persist that our Western notions of what is moral are, after all, merely Western notions. Most of us may be fairly clear about what we think to be good or bad, but, empirically speaking, has the human race really been very clear about it? A natural law

[47] Etienne Gilson, *Moral Values and the Moral Life,* trans. Leo Ward, St. Louis, 1931, pp. 200–201.

which shines with such feeble light that only a relatively few can ever see it is not much use as the basis of political or any other sort of morality; and the outlook of many is still influenced greatly by late Victorian writers who emphasized the ever-changing mores of men, the constant flux of ethical codes which were claimed merely to reflect particular cultural levels, peculiar concatenations of ecological, economic, and racial factors.[48]

But throughout the births, the migrations, and the dyings, of peoples, nations, and tribes, a fixed moral element has persisted; and in our time, a new and vigorous school of anthropology has reasserted the basic continuity of man's ethical life. With the substitution of scientific method, of "work in the field," for the armchair musings of Herbert Spencer and those benumbed by the first blasts of Darwinian theory, anthropologists have begun to insist on the abiding and common elements in the different cultures of men, the permanent human values which have guided the race so long as it has walked and fought and hunted on the earth.[49]

If the primitive savage is not to be envisioned as "endowed with lofty sentiments and exercising a passionless and calm

[48] See for example such works as: I. A. Comte, *Système de politique positive*, 4 vols., Paris, 1851–1854; J. B. Crozier, *Civilization and Progress*, London, 1885; Herbert Spencer, *The Principles of Sociology*, 3 vols., London, 1876–1896; *Social Statics*, London, 1851; *The Study of Sociology*, 9th ed., London, 1881; William Graham Sumner, *Folkways*, Boston, 1906; E. B. Tylor, *Primitive Culture*, 2 vols., London, 1871.

[49] A vast literature has grown up on the subject. See for example, Alexander A. Goldenweiser, *Early Civilization*, New York, 1922; Otto Karrer, *Religions of Mankind*, trans. E. I. Watkin, London, 1936; A. L. Kroeber, *Anthropology*, New York, 1923; Robert H. Lowie, *Primitive Society*, New York, 1921, and *An Introduction to Cultural Anthropology*, New York, 1934; W. H. R. Rivers, *History and Ethnology*, London, 1922; Wilhelm Schmidt, *The Origin and Growth of Religion*, trans. H. J. Rose, London, 1931; Wilson D. Wallis, *An Introduction to Anthropology*, New York, 1926, and *Culture and Progress*, New York, 1930.

reason in discovering the best rules of human conduct," [50] it remains a fact that man, no matter on what cultural level, is potentially a reasoning animal, and has on the whole preserved certain basic principles of individual and collective conduct. Modern authorities list many examples of such uniformity in the spheres of religion, sexual relations, barter and exchange, warfare, family and tribal life, intertribal contacts, and politics.[51] Human nature may be weak, and it is true that nowhere do we find anything like perfect observance of moral codes. The essential point is that such codes exist, largely similar to each other in their basic elements and influencing to some extent the conduct of all except a few chronic amoralists. Only in periods of moral breakdown like the present, or in areas of moral retrogression where isolated peoples or tribes may be mired in an accumulation of superstition and corrupt practice, is there a large-scale repudiation or perversion of the hard core of universal morality. Most significantly, however, it has generally been true that

as knowledge, sensibility and non-attachment increase, the contents of the judgements of value passed even by men belonging to dissimilar cultures, tend to approximate. The ethical doctrines taught in the Tao Te Ching, by Gotama Buddha and his followers of the Lesser and above all of the Greater Vehicle, in the Sermon on the Mount and by the best of the Christian Saints, are not dissimilar. Among human beings who have reached a certain level of civilization and of personal freedom from passion and social prejudice there exists a real *consensus gentium* in regard to ethical first principles.[52]

[50] T. J. Lawrence, *The Principles of International Law,* 4th ed., London, 1913, p. 37.
[51] See writers cited in note 49, above.
[52] Aldous Huxley, *Ends and Means,* London and New York, 1937, p. 282. See also Christopher Dawson, *Progress and Religion,* New York, 1928, pp. 24–177, 234–250; Otto Karrer, *op. cit.,* pp. 84 ff.
   This is not to deny the observed fact that high and noble types of moral codes may be found among extremely primitive peoples.

Now if the most purely rational men are those most likely
to agree on ethical first principles, the corollary follows that
there are ethical principles which can rationally be agreed
upon. The relativist criticism collapses in the face of comparative
study of ethical systems in their higher manifestations. An examination of the Indian concept of *dharma*, for example, will
show that the basic idea of natural law itself is common to such
seemingly disparate cultures as the Hindu and the Graeco-
Western.[53] Even the distinctive Hindu concept of *ahimsa* or
non-violence, while admittedly presenting difficulties, need not
necessarily be viewed, when taken in its proper context, as a
conspicuous exception to the unity of fundamental ethical
thought.[54] The claim is not made that all men, or even the
noblest of men, have always arrived at the same moral conclusions, but that, in their analysis of right and wrong, allowing
for differences in culture, philosophical development, and physical, social and economic environment, the great historical
ethical systems in their highest expressions tend to approximate
one another in their approach to the formulation of principles
and in many of the primary principles formulated. When an
important dissimilarity exists, it will be found to rise either out
of differing interpretations of circumstance, cause or effect, or
out of a temporary failure on one part to provide for one or
more of those prerequisites to sound ethical theory which we
discussed in Chapter IV.

The whole question of the natural law's knowability merges
into that of its *universality*, for unless the law applies to all men
under the same circumstances, it is absurd to expect them to

[53] As Dr. Beni Prasad has noted, "Classical Europe fastened on the Law
of Nature as a natural, universal law of reason implanted as a principle of
life in all hearts. Early in India there arose a similar idea which runs
through the whole of Indian philosophy and literature." *The Theory of
Government in Ancient India*, Allahabad, India, 1927, p. 18.
[54] See below, pp. 105 ff.

reach the same ethical conclusions under those circumstances. All natural law principles are universal in those cases where they apply, and apply universally when those cases arise; but, of course, only the broadest principles of being apply universally to all cases at all times and in all circumstances. In other words, the natural law is the same in Podunk Junction and Timbuctoo, the same for Adolf Hitler and Caspar Milquetoast; but different natural law principles will apply to different cases. "Always the same principle for the same case, but never a different principle because of man or place."

The law of nature is also universal in that it extends to all of man's activities, in relation to himself, his Creator, other men, and the external physical world—even if only to stipulate that a certain action is morally indifferent. There are no gaps in the great ethical scheme.

Finally, there is the property of *immutability*, a term which badly explained or wrongly understood might well create prejudice against the law of nature. In a general sense "the natural law is unchangeable because man's nature is unchangeable." [55] To stop with that, however, is to hang up a frame without any picture in it. *Immutability* is a stiff, unbending word, which may be taken to apply to something completely static, unalterably opposed to any principle of progress, growth, or change. Professor Ernst Troeltsch has, as a matter of fact, not hesitated to charge that the idea of social reform was completely absent from scholastic natural law ethics. [56] And if medieval "social reform simply meant the struggle for the Church and for Natural Law," and "did not mean that Society was to be remoulded on the lines of radical Christian thought, but that a

[55] T. Lincoln Bouscaren, "Law: Eternal, Natural, Civil," *The Modern Schoolman*, XVII (1939), 10.
[56] *The Social Teaching of the Christian Churches*, trans. Olive Wyon, 2 vols., New York, 1931, I, 303–305.

comparatively satisfactory condition was stabilized, and that the relative natural values of Society were exalted to the rank of the absolute supernatural values of the Church," [57] then scholastic theory was indeed an arid waste, akin to the sterile natural law concept of American constitutional law.

The actualities of life never achieve the ideal. But while the schoolmen sensed perhaps too vividly the peril to all values in vast social upheaval and preferred a slow gradualism to violent change, while they clung perhaps too closely to academic halls rather than marching into the highways and byways to lead popular reform movements (the perennial tragedy of the speculative thinker who seldom can be both philosopher and man of action at the same time), while on occasion they succumbed to the peril, inherent in concentration on abstract thought, of ignoring the complexities of the social dynamic, it is a gross distortion of scholastic natural law theory to identify it with a reactionary defense of the *status quo* and prevailing injustice. Whether or not, as some have claimed, Aristotle made the natural law tantamount to the established order of existing society while only Plato, among the ancients, may have conceived it as "ideal criterion for correcting existing law," [58] it remains a historical fact that the medieval form of the theory, along with its modern derivatives, has often been the inspiration and justification of political and social change. For the

natural-law theory of the State was a guide to all the political efforts and struggles from which the modern State proceeds. It is true that

[57] *Ibid.*, p. 304.
[58] Georges Gurvitch, "Natural Law," *Encyclopedia of the Social Sciences*, Vol. XI, (New York, 1938), pp. 284–290. Such an interpretation of Aristotle's viewpoint, however, hardly seems consistent with his use of the word "natural," and his discussion of the potentiality of development in man. For an acute discussion of this point see Ernest Barker, Translator's Introduction, p. xxxv, in Otto von Gierke, *Natural Law and the Theory of Society*, 2 vols., Cambridge, England, 1934.

speculation was also affected by action, and that every development of the world of thought of this period, was an echo and reverberation of historical events. But the history was never purely passive. On the contrary, it served as a pioneer in preparing the transformation of human life; it forged the intellectual arms for the struggle of new social forces; it disseminated ideas which, long before they even approached realisation, found admittance into the thought of influential circles, and became in that way, the objects of practical effort.[59]

By its very definition, the natural law should not be a passive, sterile thing, but a sensitive instrument attuned by a necessary resonance to the ever-changing panorama of human existence. Its norm of action is the nature of man, but the nature of man is not eternally bound to a specific culture or state of moral growth. Though he never basically changes, man develops new potentialities as well as realizing those which he already has; and if his historical path, in the order of actual conduct, has not been one of uniform upward progress, the residuum of perfected ethical principles, of exalted ethical ideals, in the order of knowledge, has grown with the passing of the centuries. Modern amoralists may deny the binding force of this code, but at least it is there for them to deny.

In achieving their great synthesis, the medieval scholastics added to the Peripatetic and Stoic tradition that of the Church Fathers, who by developing the teaching of Seneca that "one at least of the precepts of natural law was changed by the appearance of sin in the world and that natural law now sanctions,

[59] Otto von Gierke, *op. cit.*, I, 35. It may be added that, although most eighteenth century natural law theory was blighted as theory by the "state of nature" concept, its specific content of functional precepts derived directly from the older medieval law of nature. Some American examples of the use of natural law for a revolutionary purpose may be found in James Otis, *The Rights of the British Colonies Asserted and Proved* (pamphlet), Boston, 1764, p. 37; *Declaration of Independence*, paragraph 2; and William Lloyd Garrison, *Selections from the Writings of Garrison*, Boston, 1852, p. 66.

as expedient to sinful men, institutions that it would not have sanctioned had men continued in perfection," further emphasized the point that changing circumstances may demand changing institutions and laws.[60] There are the great primary principles, such as do good and avoid evil, which never change, intrinsically or extrinsically, materially or formally, in tropical or arctic clime, in success or failure, defeat or triumph, storm or calm—*quod semper, quod ubique*. They are static by the fitness inherent in the very nature of reality, and no man of good will wants to see them changed. The great medieval controversy between voluntarism and intellectualism found a focal point in precisely the question whether God Himself could change these apparently eternal principles of right order.[61]

Beyond this central core of justice, there are additional precepts which never change in the normal course of events, but which are not so bound up with the ultimate rationality of the universe that they cannot conceivably be altered in special cases.[62] Moreover, though the matter of these never changes, nor their expression as a specific prohibition or command relative to a certain type of action, they are not so broad and general as to apply to all phases of conduct. In other words, the "natural

[60] See Ewart Lewis, "Natural Law and Expediency in Medieval Political Theory," *Ethics*, L (1940), 146.

[61] Extreme voluntarism finds an interesting parallel in the modern totalitarian reaction to the arid mechanistic materialism and empirical "scientificism" of the past 100 years, reflecting, in a sense, that general tendency to react to an overstern rationalism by exalting the will at the expense of all objective normative standards. *In medias res stat virtus*, but the fate of man apparently destines him to swing pendulum-like from one extreme to the other. See Morehouse F. X. Millar, S.J., "Scholasticism and American Political Philosophy," in John Zybura, *Present-Day Thinkers and the New Scholasticism*, St. Louis, 1926, pp. 325–326. See also William Turner, *History of Philosophy*, Boston, 1929, pp. 390 ff. for a discussion of the voluntarist position and citation of leading works.

[62] The classic examples are the permitting of polygamy in the case of the patriarchs, and the granting of divorce to the Israelites under the Old Law. See Ignatius Cox, *op. cit.*, pp. 91–92.

law discerns the mutability contained in the subject matter" of moral principles, and "adapts its own precepts to this mutability, prescribing . . . a certain sort of conduct for one condition, and another sort of conduct for another condition." [63]

Finally, there are merely permissive or concessive principles, of which not only the subject matter may change; with changing circumstances, these principles may themselves change.[64]

The upshot of such a schema is no rigid code of straitjacketing rules, but a flexible, workable ethical system. After all, the great, universally applicable, general principles are relatively few in comparison to the manifold secondary and only particularly applicable principles of action in all phases of social and individual life. While the law of nature viewed as a whole is a hierarchical structure of norms, each subordinate to and consistent with the one above it, all these norms are subordinate to the end towards which they are the rationally necessary means and from which they derive their validity.

Such a system may, in a sense, be described as a "thoroughgoing relativism in the application of natural law norms to positive laws and institutions," as "affirming inviolable ends for mankind but allowing the utmost flexibility in the choice of means." [65] It is the only workable utilitarianism, for it specifies a goal towards which action is to be useful—but it is definitely not the same as saying that the end justifies the means. The scholastic tradition is entirely against the use of bad means to attain a worthy end, and utmost flexibility in the choice of means exists only within the scope of permissible means. A caution is also necessary against going to the extreme of Professor Chester Maxey when he writes that St. Thomas' "concep-

---

[63] Francisco Suárez, *Tractatus de Legibus ac Deo Legislatore*, II, iii. See also Aquinas, *Summa Theologica*, I–II, 94, 5; Viktor Cathrein, *op. cit.*, pp. 403 ff.; Joseph Rickaby, *op. cit.*, p. 371; Albert Valensin, *op. cit.*, p. 197.
[64] See Francisco Suárez, *op. cit.*   [65] Ewart Lewis, *op. cit.*, pp. 149, 163.

tion of natural law does not pre-suppose the existence of universal and immutable canons of right reason, but rather a body of rational precepts which may change and grow as human reason and human institutions undergo change and development." [66] Such a view apparently fails to realize the need, upon which all the great schoolmen insisted, for a sound metaphysical basis for all thought and a central core of immutable principle for all ethical thought.

A truly creative natural law opens the way for the achievement of justice in human law, which is free to change in order to meet the needs of the day and age, in fact must change to meet those needs if it is to remain compatible with natural law. Such a natural law can provide the man of good will with a valid basis both for his good will and the objectives which he desires. In the sphere of power, its general acceptance would insure that ethical control which is so essential. The extended discussion which follows in Chapters VI and VII attempts to make specific and detailed application of the functional, natural law approach to the two most important moral as well as practical aspects of the problem of power: the role of violence, and the relationship of authority's power to the claim of liberty. It will become clear, we believe, that such application is not only possible and valid, but that its suppositions are implicit in any satisfactory resolution of the problem.

[66] *Political Philosophies*, New York, 1938, p. 118.

VI

The Function of Violence

To THOSE who feel that peace between men is the ideal condition of society, there is something of permanent appeal in the thought of conquering violence by non-violence, of overcoming physical power by the power of non-violence. Though often in the past its most prominent defenders have been detached individuals like Thoreau or Tolstoy living apart from the main stream of Western mores and thought, or the adherents of minority sects like the Quakers and Mennonites, the pacifist claim that only on the path of non-violence can a solution to the problem of power be found has not lacked eloquent advocacy in our day. And if it be true that "individual experience and a study of history, past and contemporary" prove that "the most effective, the most equitable, the most economical way of meeting violence is to use non-violence," [1] then indeed the role of non-violence deserves more than supercilious acknowledgment in a power-ridden age.

While men of good will have consistently denied that might makes right, they have usually admitted that might may enforce right, that it may be the lesser of two evils physically to coerce or even to kill provided that a more important value is preserved or defended. But does this approach involve a basic fallacy? Does the use of physical force, of violence, always prove essentially futile, either in that it usually fails to achieve its in-

[1] Aldous Huxley, *An Encyclopedia of Pacifism*, New York, 1937, p. 64.

tended effect, or in that the same effect could have been achieved more effectively, more equitably and more economically by the use of non-violent means? Needless to say, an affirmative answer to these questions has far-reaching implications which require radical revision of certain traditional concepts of the role of public authority and the legitimacy of the use of force to support that authority.

To many of its advocates, non-violence is not merely the best way to control power in a pragmatic sense; it is a general precept of conduct, a basic tenet of a moral code which bans the use of physical force. It involves an entire philosophy of life, which in our time has found eloquent expression in such writers as Aldous Huxley and Richard Gregg. With the exception of the pacifist Christian sects, virtually all modern exponents of non-violence in the West have been influenced to a greater or lesser extent by Indian thought with its doctrine of non-violence, which many regard as the distinctive contribution of India to ethical theory and to the control of power.[2] In its twentieth century form, as expounded by Mohandas Gandhi and his followers, it has generally received sympathetic appreciation if not practice in the West; and a recent attempt like that of Krishnalal Shridharani to describe the theory and practice of non-violence elicited much favorable comment, with even eminent university professors breaking out into recommendations enthusiastic enough to serve as blurbs on the book jacket.[3]

While certain Indian writers have recognized a legitimate use of force,[4] the doctrine of absolute non-violence has through-

---

[2] See Sir Charles Eliot, *Hinduism and Buddhism*, 2 vols. London, 1921, II, 170; E. W. Hopkins, *Ethics of India*, New Haven, Conn., 1924, pp. 232–233.
[3] See *War without Violence*, New York, 1939.
[4] See for example, *Santi Parva*, 16, 67; *Adi Purana*, XVI, 252; *Manu Samhita*, VII, 20; *Arthasastra*, trans. Sama Shastry, Mysore, 1909, pp. 10, 26.

out the centuries held a peculiar fascination for the Indian mind. Some knowledge of the philosophical background to the Satyagraha movement of Gandhi is absolutely essential for those who would understand its strength in India, and as a source of restraint for those who would attempt the unqualified transfer to the West of a highly interrelated system of distinctive concepts and doctrines. For only in the intellectual atmosphere of Hindu India, deriving from many centuries of common tradition, culture, and philosophy, could a modern movement based on non-violence have achieved such efficacy and popular appeal. This is not to deny what Gandhi himself acknowledged—his ideological debt to Tolstoy and Thoreau [5]—but merely to underline the fact that Gandhi succeeded in establishing a mass movement based on his teachings whereas both Tolstoy and Thoreau remained to the end lone voices crying in the wilderness.

Of primary importance in the making of the modern theory of Satyagraha is the ancient Indian doctrine of *ahimsa*. In the background of its formulation and development is that basic philosophy of Hindu as well as of Buddhist and Jainist India, which has molded the people of the country to a unique outlook and attitude of mind, and which, in its highest forms, is so expressive of the nobler aspects of the Indian character and tradition. The meaning of *ahimsa* is simply this: to refrain from hurting any other being with "mind, body and speech." [6] It involves not only abstention from the infliction of harm but the abandoning of any wish to do so. Its scope, moreover, is not limited to human beings but extends to all being.

[5] Especially Tolstoy's *The Kingdom of God Is within You*, New York, 1894; and Thoreau's *Essay on Civil Disobedience*, first published in *Aesthetic Papers*, Boston, 1849, and included in *Anti-Slavery and Reform Papers*, selected and edited by H. S. Salt, London, 1890.
[6] Nigamananda, *Yogiguru*, Calcutta, (n.d.), p. 58.

Contrary to what might seem the logical process, the *ahimsa* injunction did not originally grow out of a feeling of compassion evoked by the suffering in this world. Its original purpose, in fact, was quite the opposite: to assist in the elimination of all feeling, of all emotion and appetence, in order to achieve release (*moksa*) not only from the woes of this mundane life but from existence itself. The essential thought behind this negativism in its early Brahmanic and Jainist forms is that the perpetuation of conscious individual existence is an evil and that release consists in the cessation of such existence. *Ahimsa* is part of a general withdrawal from participation in life; its ultimate purpose is the cessation of all activity, mental or physical, through which existence manifests itself. Violence and force, the quest for power, are strong expressions of human desire and activity. Non-violence, on the other hand, requires not only the absence of activity with respect to an immediate object but also a purging of the emotions and of the will to action. One might think that logically such an attitude should lead to the advocacy, along with George Eliot in a moment of Victorian despair, of "one grand simultaneous act of suicide" as the only course for the human race. Such a conclusion was, however, never generally reached; and Indian negativism was soon tempered by other developments, including the new doctrines of *karma* and transmigration which made the ending of existence a process quite apart from that mere physical ending of a particular life which suicide could achieve.

Men being what they are, a purely formal and non-ethical concept of *ahimsa* could scarcely endure. A positive ethical note began to creep in at an early stage, though apparently inconsistent with a philosophy which sought release in the cessation of existence deriving not from the observance of moral precepts but from the elimination of all activity. It was probably Buddha himself who first introduced the element of compassion or sympathy into the *ahimsa* principle, and the spreading influence of his teachings generalized this new spirit even among the Brahmans. *Ahimsa* soon became not merely a moral precept relative to the use of force, but the highest *dharma*, the fundamental virtue, the standard by which judgment may be passed on all actions. Through the full practice of *ahimsa*, the seeker of truth finds *moksa*. The great thinkers of the classical period in Indian philosophy added little to this aspect of ethical theory as emphasis tended to shift to other levels of conduct,[7] but the *ahimsa* doctrine continued throughout the centuries to exercise a certain formative influence in the molding of the Indian outlook.[8]

Aside from its debt to this original doctrine of non-violence, the modern Satyagraha movement derives part of its ideology and spirit from the distinctive doctrine of *tapas*. According to the latter, which is illustrated by numerous stories in the ancient literature of India, a man may acquire power over other men, or even over the gods, by the practice of renunciation and self-mortification through which he amasses reserves of supernatural power sufficient to achieve his objective. What Lord

[7] It may be noted in passing that the tendency among early students to describe all mature Indian thought in terms of complete negativism has been shown to be inaccurate by more recent research.

[8] The literature on the subject of Indian philosophies and religions, as well as the number of original texts now available in English translation, has grown to enormous proportions. We can cite here only a few of the most useful general surveys: (the Vedas) M. Winternitz, *A History of Indian Literature*, trans. S. Ketkar, Calcutta, 1927, I, 47–196, and A. A. Macdonell, *Sanskrit Literature*, London, 1900, pp. 40–170; (the Upanishads) Paul Deussen, *Philosophy of the Upanishads*, Edinburgh, 1906, and Winternitz, *op. cit.*, pp. 226–310; (Buddhism) Louis de la Vallée Poussin, *Bouddhisme; opinions sur l'histoire de la dogmatique*, Paris, 1909, and *The Way to Nirvana*, Cambridge, 1917; (Jainism) Winternitz, *op. cit.*, II, Calcutta, 1933, 424–615; (the Epics) E. W. Hopkins, *The Great Epic of India*, New York, 1901; (the Philosophies) P. Johanns, *Vers le Christ par le Vedanta*, Louvain, 1932; S. Radhakrishnan, *Indian Philosophy*, London, 2d ed., 1931, Vol. II.

Ronaldshay has called the classic example of the practice of *tapas* is found in the story of Visvamitra, a well-known figure of the Hindu *Vedas*, *Epics*, and *Puranas*. Through the practice of austerities he eventually acquires such power as actually to become a menace even to the gods, and he is persuaded to desist from his course only through the intervention of Brahma who grants him the rank of Brahmanhood.[9]

The concept of *tapas* was part of the general early Hindu theory of sacrifice which, based on a strict *do ut des* (I give that you may give) motivation, stipulated that once the required sacrifices were duly performed, the desired reward automatically followed. The implication was not merely of a genial godhead willing always to carry out its part of an implied contract, but of a cosmic nature and its forces which could be evoked by incantations and magic formulae. In the words of Dr. Heimann, "All expended energy is regarded as concrete substance which, when directed to some object of devotion, increases its force, thus enabling, and indeed compelling, it to achieve adequate counteraction." [10]

The Satyagraha movement has in its theoretical background these traditional Indian doctrines of *ahimsa* and *tapas*, which are not mere lifeless abstractions but living beliefs. To them Gandhi added certain positive elements both in the development of a detailed methodology of non-violence and in the identification of Satyagraha with the conquering power of truth.[11]

[9] See the Earl of Ronaldshay, *The Heart of Aryavarta*, London, 1925, pp. 5–6. See also Winternitz, *op. cit.*, I, 402 ff., 480.
[10] *Indian and Western Philosophy*, London, 1937, p. 73.
[11] For the American reader, Krishnalal Shridharani's *War without Violence*, while somewhat uncritical, is perhaps the best general discussion of the techniques of Satyagraha. His treatment of the theoretical background to the movement is, however, inadequate and misleading. Gandhi's own writings provide, of course, a voluminous source of detail and exposition (see references in following footnotes).

Gandhi variously defined Satyagraha as "holding on to truth," "truth force," "love-force or soul force"; [12] and he deliberately coined the term in order to distinguish his early movement in South Africa from mere passive resistance.[13] He claimed that non-violence is not "passivity in any shape or form" and that the *ahimsa* commandment can be fulfilled only by the complete practice of love,[14] which quality is called the "law of our being," [15] "the supreme and only law of life." [16] Perhaps the most precise attempt at definition is to be found in the Constitution of the Gandhi Seva Sangh, an association of Gandhi followers, which notes that

The expression "the principles of Satyagraha as laid down in the teachings of Mahatma Gandhi" means an eternal and humble search after Truth through the ever-progressive practice in thought, word and deed of the following and allied means of realizing it, viz., Non-violence, which included love, control of the senses, non-possession, non-covetousness, freedom from fear, control of the palate, bread labour, neighborliness (Swadeshi), removal of untouchability and conception of high and low, equal regard for all religions, and resistance of evil through good.[17]

In this meaning, non-violence is an all-inclusive principle of action (as it was to the ancient Hindus), which itself is the way of truth, the means of realizing truth, the "external face of truth." [18]

The Gandhian "truth" is obviously not restricted to our customary use of the term as the conformity of objective reality

[12] See collection of statements by Gandhi defining Satyagraha in B. Pattabhi Sitaramayya's *Gandhi and Gandhism*, Allahabad, 1942, I, 100 ff.
[13] *Ibid.*
[14] See *Harijan* (Poona), March 14, 1936; Oct. 17, 1936; Dec. 17, 1938; Sept. 15, 1940.
[15] *Ibid.*, Sept. 26, 1936.   [16] *Ibid.*, April 13, 1940.
[17] *Constitution of Gandhi Seva Sangh*, note to Section 1 (a).
[18] See *Young India* (Ahmedabad), May 20, 1926. See also Sitaramayya, *op. cit.*, pp. 97 ff.

to that which is said or thought about it.[19] It is conceived as a positive force [20]—hence the expression "truth-force"—the possession of which gives to those who practice Satyagraha a power which must in the end triumph. The power of violence is controlled first by non-violent resistance, which in turn leads to the conversion to truth of those who abuse power and the elimination of violence as a means of achieving objectives among all parties concerned. This belief in the inevitability of the triumph of "truth," which is a frequently recurring theme in Gandhi's writings, is not, of course, subject to proof in terms of familiar Western concepts, but derives much of its basic conviction from the traditional Indian theory of acquiring power through suffering, renunciation, and the growth of soul-force.

It should be clear therefore that the Indian philosophy of non-violence is more than just another variety of pacifism as the term is used in the West. It embodies a distinctive world outlook some of the basic concepts of which may well appear unacceptable to the Western mind. But that does not in itself mean that the practice of non-violence cannot be advocated in terms more familiar to Western political thought. One may consider, as does Shridharani, that "as a form of mass action directed toward the attainment of desired social ends, Satyagraha is just another technique which mankind can use at will," with no claim to moral superiority; although how it is to pass the test of "higher efficiency" divorced from the ideological sources of that faith and fervor necessary to make it work he leaves without satisfactory explanation.[21]

Or, more justifiably, it can be contended that there are certain elements of universal validity in the philosophy of non-violence

[19] This is a popular definition of course; the metaphysician distinguishes between ontological truth, logical truth and moral truth.
[20] *Young India*, Dec. 31, 1931.
[21] See *War without Violence*, pp. 314 ff.

which can be abstracted from any specific national or cultural context. Perhaps the most eloquent defense of this viewpoint in our time may be found in the writings of Aldous Huxley, whose arguments deserve more consideration than they often get. How shallow many of his critics actually are may be gathered from the frequent derisive references to Huxley as purveyor of a brand of "Hollywood Buddhism." Such inept labeling could proceed only from ignorance of Buddhism as well as Huxley, who is much closer in thought to the great Indian philosopher Samkara than to Buddha. Nor can Huxley simply be dismissed as another of those "hacks of Yogi-journalese" to whom Arthur Koestler so contemptuously refers.[22] He poses certain basic questions, and gives answers, relating to the problem of power and the use of violence which political scientists must consider and evaluate. Is the use of physical force, of violence, ever legitimate in the achievement of objectives considered desirable by the man of good will? If not, can those objectives always be achieved by non-violent means?

Reduced to its bare components, the argument for non-violence is essentially this: [23] Violence is always relatively inefficient and cannot by itself lead to any real progress. It can produce only the effects of violence, which are "counter-violence, suspicion and resentment on the part of the victims and the creation, among the perpetrators, of a tendency to use more violence"; and these effects can be undone only by compensatory and reparatory acts of non-violence, acts of justice and good will, after the event.[24] Non-violence has throughout history, even though used sporadically and unsystematically,

[22] *The Yogi and the Commissar*, p. 246.
[23] See Aldous Huxley, *Ends and Means*, London and New York, 1937, especially Chaps. IV, IX, X, XIV.
[24] *Ibid.*, p. 25.

proved that it can overcome evil and turn aside anger and hatred; while the use of violence has left a long record of frustration and perversion of ideals. Common sense demands, therefore, that we "begin with non-violence and not run the risk of stultifying" a whole process "by using violence, even as an initial measure." [25] But in addition to its proved pragmatic value, non-violence also rests on a valid philosophical basis and "is the practical consequence that follows from belief in the fundamental unity of all being." [26]

THE MORALITY OF FORCE

Anyone who maintains that force still has a legitimate role to play in modern society must guard against giving the impression that violence per se is ever good and desirable. To the moral man, a discussion of the function of violence should be both realistic and unenthusiastic. It can be established, we believe, that the facts of social and political life are still such as to make the use of violence necessary, under certain limited circumstances, in order to achieve an objective the non-achievement of which would constitute a greater evil than that involved in such use of violence. But the need for violence is just as regrettable as the existence of those facts which necessitate it, and any exaltation or joy in its use is a definite perversity. The whole subject is a delicate one which the moralist and the political scientist must approach with clear concepts, exact definitions, and close reasoning.

Is violence always relatively inefficient? Obviously not always for those who use it with evil purpose. But is violence used in a worthy cause, for a good end, always less effective than non-violence would be under the same circumstances? A worthy cause may mean either self-defense pure and simple, or some

[25] *Ibid.*, p. 126.   [26] *Ibid.*, p. 140.

positive reform to be effected. If a robber comes at a man with a knife and definite intent to kill, the person assailed is hardly likely to have much doubt about the relative efficacy of a pistol in his hand and passive resistance. In such a case violence would not only be relatively most efficient; it is the only thing that would work at all in the defense of an individual life. Most men will readily admit that actual situations can arise in which the defense of an individual or a group requires the use of violence.

In the sphere of what Huxley calls "large-scale social reform" the utility of violence is not so evident. The fact, upon which he lays so much emphasis, that violence cannot lead to real progress unless it is followed by compensatory acts of non-violence does not in itself prove that violence is never necessary. It simply means that by itself violence is not enough; it may, however, be an indispensable prerequisite to progress. It is true that violence is always dangerous, for a habit of violence is easily formed, and all too often violence begets more violence. But the possibility of abuse does not automatically preclude use; there must also be a better way to achieve the same desirable and proportionate result before we can say that violence should not be used.

Discussion of the relative pragmatic value of violence and non-violence can continue indefinitely, and we shall have to clarify further aspects of this question in attempting to state certain general principles which must be considered in the formulation of a sound morality of power. But the advocate of non-violence does not usually base his case purely on its alleged superiority in the working order. To him non-violence is likely to be an absolute precept of morality deriving, it is claimed, from the philosophical doctrine of the unity of being.[27]

[27] Some persons, of course, espouse various degrees of pacifism for other reasons, such as a particular interpretation of the Christian teaching, or

The fundamental moral commandment is that men should realize their unity with all being, and, in order to realize this unity, men must practice the virtues of love and understanding, of non-violence. "Ultimate reality is impersonal and non-ethical; but if we would realize our true relations with ultimate reality and our fellow-beings, we must practice morality and (since no personality can learn to transcend itself unless it is reasonably free from external compulsion) respect the personality of others." [28]

Now no matter what name we give to a philosophy based on the hypothesis of the fundamental unity of all being, inevitably it is subject to the same basic criticism as any monistic concept of reality. This is not the place for a lengthy analysis of the metaphysical difficulties of monism—in the present case a pantheistic monism—or of its negative implication for ethics. The task has been ably done by others.[29] Suffice it to say here that a study of the history of philosophy will show that any positive ethical theory in monistic systems has derived not from monism but from extraneous concepts, often basically incompatible with monism or representing a deviation from or modification of pure monism. Huxley's discussion is weakest on this point, and one cannot help but feel that he has not fully grasped the essential issues involved. Mere realization of unity has no significance unless interpreted in terms which give that unity

---

an economic theory which makes out all wars to be nothing but a form of economic exploitation.

[28] Aldous Huxley, *op. cit.*, pp. 300–301.

[29] Among modern writers see for example, P. Coffey, *Ontology*, London, 1914, p. 46 *passim*; Adolph von Harnack, *What Is Christianity?*, 3d ed., trans. Thomas Bailey Saunders, London, 1904, pp. 153 ff.; George Hayward Joyce, S.J., *Principles of Natural Theology*, London, 1924, pp. 481 ff.; W. S. Urquhart, *Pantheism and the Value of Life*, Oxford, 1925, *passim*; E. I. Watkin, *A Philosophy of Form*, New York, 1935, pp. 190 ff., 286 ff.

value. Knowing that we are made of the same essential substance as rocks will not make us love rocks; logically, no more
will it make us love men. The basis of love for our fellow men
is not mere identity of being, but realization of our common
human nature sharing a common and higher ethical purpose.

The argument that we must practice morality to achieve
unity with "non-ethical" ultimate reality runs into the same
logical impasse that plagued the early Buddhists and certain of
the Vedantists when they attempted to combine an ethic of
compassion with a philosophy of world-negation. The inevitable
development led either to the nihilism of Nagarjuna and Guada-
pada,[30] the introduction of personal and ethical deities,[31] or a
reversion to the pure Brahmanism of Samkara.[32] The latter
realized, as Mr. Huxley does not, that a personal ethics of love
is irrelevant in a system of monistic world-negation, and that
the realization of unity with impersonal being requires an essentially negative rather than a positive approach. Escape from
desire and existence, pursued with single-mindedness, is a goal
to be achieved by a form of quietist meditation and not by good
works.[33]

No matter how well-intentioned, Mr. Huxley's plea for non-
violence as a means to nothing will have little appeal for the
generality of men, just as the rarefied speculations of Samkara
have failed to attract the masses of India or to influence their
essential beliefs and codes. Men will not be satisfied with a

---

[30] See Winternitz, op. cit., II, 341 ff.; also Louis de la Vallée Poussin,
Bouddhisme, Opinions sur l'Histoire de la Dogmatique, pp. 189 ff.; and
W. S. Urquhart, The Vedanta and Modern Thought, Oxford, 1928, pp.
46 ff.
[31] See Nicol Macnicol, Indian Theism, Oxford, 1915, pp. 62 ff.
[32] See G. Dandoy, S.J., L'Ontologie du Vedanta, Paris, 1932, pp. 99 ff.;
Olivier LaCombe, L'Absolu selon le Vedanta, Paris, 1937, passim; W. S.
Urquhart, op. cit., pp. 73 ff.
[33] See W. S. Urquhart, op. cit., pp. 172–190.

handful of negatives, and an ethical system in which the doing of good is a virtue having positive significance can only derive from a philosophy which recognizes the relation of desire to purpose and provides for its ultimate fulfillment and not extinction. That the role of ethics is to ordain the desires and conduct of men in accordance with the functional order of being, so that men may find happiness, is recognized in both the natural law theory of the West and the *dharma* theory of India; both provide a basis of morality consistent with the best in human nature without denying the value of its existence or aspirations.

Who is entitled to use physical force? Every individual not completely paralyzed can exert such force to a greater or lesser extent, and even in the small everyday activities of men it is an important factor in getting things done, though it may involve only killing a mosquito or shutting a door. While such uses of physical force may have ethical significance as means to a good or bad purpose behind a course of action, we are here primarily concerned with those cases of physical force, actual or threatened, which involve the coercion of other human beings. The modern advocate of absolute non-violence regards all such uses of force as immoral, but is unable to justify his position in terms of a positive code deriving logically from a basic philosophy of value. While he can often make a strong case in a given set of circumstances, when he attempts to argue for non-violence purely on the ground of greater relative efficiency, he is unable to prove that non-violence is always more efficient than violence under all circumstances, a claim which runs counter to common sense and the ordinary experience of men. As a matter of fact, faced with the realities of political and social life, he may at times waver himself. Thus after a review of certain historical attempts at "large-scale social reform" which, he alleges, were vitiated by the use of violence, Mr. Huxley comes to this rather surprising conclusion: "If, then, we wish to make large-scale reforms which will not stultify ourselves in the process of application, we must choose our measures in such a way that no violence, or, at the worst, very little violence will be needed to enforce them." [34]

Few will quarrel with such a statement, which, however, is scarcely consistent with Huxley's general position. For once the legitimacy of even "a very little violence" is admitted, the entire theoretical structure of non-violence collapses. If non-violence is not an absolute principle of conduct but merely a desirable means when it works, it acquires significance only as part of a system of ethical values which determines when it is desirable and when it is not. Else where draw the line in a specific case between the "very little violence" that is permissible and the violence that is immoral?

There are three essential types of conflict which may lead to the use of physical force: between individual and individual, between individual and association, and between association and association. Within these general categories we may, of course, further classify the various kinds of conflict according to the numbers involved and the locus of initiative. Thus the refusal of conscientious objectors to serve in the armed forces of a state or the attempt of the state to put a criminal behind bars are both examples of conflict between individual and association. The great focal point of physical power is, of course, the state— the great political association—and generally speaking, it "alone has the last resort of compulsion." [35] But individuals may use

[34] *Ends and Means*, p. 28.
[35] R. M. MacIver, *Society, Its Structure and Changes*, New York, 1931, p. 14. Professor MacIver's brilliant elucidation in his various works of the "key-words" *society, community, association*, and *institution* has made a definite contribution to clarity of sociological and political concepts and

violence against other individuals, and a discussion of the issues involved in such cases will help to clarify our approach to the larger problems of conflict.

It is axiomatic that the use of physical force against another human being is never good in itself; it can be justified only in defense of a superior right. If a would-be murderer attacks a man, the latter may certainly defend his life with all the energy he has at his disposal, and no court of law or moralist will condemn him even if he kills his assailant in the legitimate process of self-defense. Yet the "unnatural" death of the murderer, no matter how wicked and depraved a person he may have been, is an evil, not a good result. How then justify the use of violence in self-defense without falling into the fallacy of arguing that the end justifies the means—even the use of evil means?

Now the refusal to admit that a good end does not justify the use of evil means does not imply that, in a situation where only two alternatives exist, both of them evil and one or the other of them necessary, a person may not choose the lesser of two evils. If one does not so choose, then the greater evil inevitably prevails. A good as well as an evil result follows from the act of self-defense. It is a clear-cut case of conflict of rights: the right of the person attacked to his life and the right of the assailant to his life. Of the two, the former's right is obviously superior. Ethically speaking, the question of intention is also important at this point. One may never, of course, intend to kill an assailant as an end in itself; the end must be the preservation of one's own right to life. Moralists speak of an *indirect voluntary* act or an act *voluntary in cause* to identify an effect that follows from the placing of a cause intended to achieve some

---

terminology. We use the term *association* in his sense of "a group specifically organized for the pursuit of an interest or group of interests in common," *Ibid.*, p. 12.

other effect. They generally agree that it is lawful to place a cause from which two effects follow, one good, the other evil, if the cause is good, or the lesser of two evils one or the other of which is necessary; if the good effect follows as immediately and directly from the cause as the evil effect; if there is a grave and proportionate reason for placing the cause; and if the good effect is directly intended and the evil effect merely permitted.[36]

These are sound natural law (which mean common sense) principles of action; they are not derived from esoteric formulae or unrealistic speculation. We can only conclude that, under certain conditions, the use of violence in blameless self-defense is ethically permissible for the individual. Just how much violence may be used depends, of course, on the actual situation in each case. If the right to life can be reasonably protected without inflicting death upon an assailant, then violence is legitimate only up to the point required to protect that right. This is not to deny that sometimes non-violence may be more effective than violence in the face of hostility and abuse, but it would take a rash person indeed to claim that passive resistance will always halt the homicidal maniac. If the case is admittedly an extreme one, it is certainly not without its equally melodramatic parallels in real life. It is unlikely that many of those who have faced Gestapo trigger-men with orders to kill, and have escaped, will claim that non-violence saved them.

The fact is that even the most uncompromising advocates of non-violence concentrate largely on the sphere of group and mass action, and fail to get down to the ethical problem of the individual faced with a great and immediate danger to his life and an urgent need to use violence in order to save it. In his

[36] Any standard scholastic treatise on ethics such as Michael J. Cronin, *The Science of Ethics*, 2 vols., New York, 1917–1920; or Henry Davis, S.J., *Moral and Pastoral Theology*, 3 vols., New York, 1935, will contain further discussion and examples of the *indirect voluntary* act.

Ends and Means, Mr. Huxley devotes a few pages to showing the "power of non-violence in the relations of individuals with individuals," but nowhere does he discuss these "either-or" cases. We can all agree that "men of exceptional moral force and even ordinary people, when strengthened by intense conviction, have demonstrated over and over again in the course of history the power of non-violence to overcome evil, to turn aside anger and hatred"; [37] but this does not prove the universal efficacy of non-violence. When it works, non-violence is always preferable to violence. When it will not work, violence may be necessary to defend a proportionate right.

With this background of principle affecting the use of violence by individuals against other individuals, we may now consider the question of violence or physical force in the relation of individual to association. Although violence may sometimes be involved in conflict between individuals and certain of the non-political associations, as, for example, in the rough handling of scab workers by the members of a striking labor union, the great problems in this category are those rising out of conflict between individuals and the state—the great political association—with its unique control of concentrated power in the police and the military, and its monopoly of so-called legal right to use physical compulsion. Men have discussed the state by mouth and in writing throughout the centuries, and have proved that a theory can be concocted to justify the need of any government bent on misusing the power of the state. It is no exaggeration to say that any theory of the state which attributes to it an absolute value in itself, apart from its value as means, can be used as part of an argument for some form of absolutism and is therefore incompatible with the ethical control of power. On the other hand, any denial to the state of the

[37] Huxley, *op. cit.*, p. 141.

right to use physical force under all circumstances must end by denying the value of the state. The moral right of the state to employ violence derives from the need for violence in carrying out its function; the state has no right in the abstract to use physical force without reference to purpose. Each ethically permissible use of violence by the state must be ordinated to a proportionately good end, the achievement of which is a legitimate function of the state. Hence any attempt to establish the moral authority of the state must begin with a clear understanding of its purpose.

There is no need to discuss here the actual historical origin of the modern state.[38] The fact is that states now exist, and may in a general sense be described as groups of people organized in political association under an autonomous government upon a definite territory. Only the anarchist and the Marxian purist will deny that their existence serves a useful and indispensable purpose, no matter now many abuses may be involved along the way. They are not mere social incubi upon the backs of men from which all would gladly escape. Men of good will can agree that, in its broadest aspect, the function of the state is to promote the general welfare, the common good, and that any state activity which goes counter to that purpose is unethical. Such men may well differ at times as to whether specific actions will contribute to the common good, and in the ideal order of things differences of this type would provide the sole basis for political opposition to the government. But once action becomes clearly necessary for the common good, they will not deny to the state the right to use sufficient power to achieve its purpose.

The state fulfills its function by providing those general conditions which are necessary to fullest achievement of good by

[38] See R. M. MacIver, *The Modern State*, Oxford, 1926, pp. 25–144; also Robert H. Lowie, *The Origin of the State*, New York, 1927; William C. MacLeod, *The Origin of the State*, Philadelphia, 1924.

free individuals, and it does this primarily through the instrument of political control known as law, or more specifically, positive law.[39] These necessary general conditions will vary from age to age, and from society to society, but they will always include the maintenance of "the universal external conditions of social order." [40] Without social order the entire fabric of complex modern life, with its constant interraction and frequent conflict between individual and individual, between group and group, would fall apart. No matter how rigid and slow to necessary change they may be, the vast bodies of established law which have developed in all civilized countries serve the essential purpose of bringing within the scope of predictable state action the basic sources of conflict and disintegration, and thus either preventing or rectifying undesirable conduct legally proscribed.

But the function of the state cannot stop with the mere maintenance of order. Many nineteenth century liberals thought of the state as a glorified and somewhat impersonal policeman with a largely or completely negative role.[41] The less government the better government! Needless to say, the decline of liberalism was not hindered by this failure to grasp the need for more positive state activity in the promotion of the common good. For the common good requires more than order, which may be the order of either the servile or the democratic state. It requires multifarious activities directed towards the achievement of justice and general happiness which the state is best fitted to perform.[42] We do not mean, of course, that the state can or should inter-

[39] See R. M. MacIver, *op. cit.*, especially Chap. III, for a lucid discussion of the role of law in the state.
[40] *Ibid.*, p. 22.
[41] See Ernest Barker, *Political Thought in England*, London and New York, 1924, Chap. IV; also John A. Ryan and Morehouse F. X. Millar, *The State and the Church*, New York, 1922, pp. 208 ff.
[42] See R. M. MacIver, *Society, Its Structure and Changes*, pp. 198 ff.

est itself in the achievement of each specific good for each specific individual. That is the claim of totalitarianism. Only within the scope of its legitimate function has the state a right to act,[43] but when it has that right it need not be inhibited by any arbitrary and more limited concept of its function than the promotion of the general welfare.

Under this purely functional view of the state, is the use of violence, of physical compulsion, a legitimate and necessary means of achieving the common good? If it were not necessary, it would not, of course, be legitimate, since state violence like individual violence is never good in itself. The ethical principles involved are much the same as in the case of individual self-defense, but the physical power of the state has a more positive role to play. It is not merely a question of the user of violence defending a superior right which he possesses; the rights which the state defends are generally those of some of its members against the encroachment of others of its members. It must protect rights, not merely when they are immediately and seriously threatened in a specific case, but by maintaining a general system of legal obligations and prohibitions, sanctioned by the power of the state, which will serve to deter those who want to deprive others of their rights and which will enable the despoiled to regain their rights. That the state can enforce law against willful transgression without the threat of, or the actual ultimate resort to, violent compulsion is a claim which few will seriously make, and which certainly does not accord with the harsh realities of human nature. It is true that "if the ethical conviction of the bindingness of law were always and universally effective, there would be no need for legal sanctions"; [44] and hence the great importance of having a philosophy

---

[43] For a discussion of the limitations of state function with particular reference to human liberty, see below, pp. 152 ff.

[44] Luigi Sturzo, *Inner Laws of Society*, New York, 1944, p. 225.

generally accepted upon which such ethical conviction can be
soundly based. But even under the best of conditions there are
always likely to be a few lawbreakers who will jeopardize the
rights of others. How are they to be dealt with?

One can, of course, take the position that the entire structure
of state-enforced law is a bad thing, and this is substantially what
anarchists like Thoreau and Kropotkin have argued.[45] Though
they may not like certain of its manifestations, most men will,
however, concede the indispensable function of law in the preservation of those conditions which make for ordered and secure
living. The advocate of non-violence may be silent on this point,
but when he follows his denial of the state's right to use violent
compulsion to its logical conclusion he can only end by taking an
essential anarchistic position. Mr. Huxley writes of a police force
"trained in non-violence" which "could use modern methods to
forestall any outbreak of violence, to prevent potential hostilities
from developing, to foster cooperation," and which "could be
made a complete substitute for an army"; [46] but his description
is singularly lacking in details as to just how such a police force
would operate as a police force. If the term means anything at
all, a police force is presumably a law-enforcing body imple-
menting the so-called "police power" of the state. It is the means
through which the state exercises internally the ultimate sanction of violence.

A common mistake is to think of this sanction of violence
largely, if not solely, in terms of criminal law enforcement. As
a matter of fact, which every law student soon discovers, the
civil law constitutes by far the largest part of the *corpus legum*.
Touching as it does upon so many aspects of commercial and

---

[45] See for example, Henry Thoreau, *Essay on Civil Disobedience;* Prince
Peter Kropotkin, *Fields, Factories and Workshops*, London, 1899, and
Memoirs of a Revolutionist, London, 1900.
[46] Huxley, *op. cit.*, p. 155n.

even domestic activity in a complex modern society, it serves as the necessary framework in the formation, development, and preservation of institutions and habits. Behind the civil law, just as behind the criminal law, is the ultimate sanction of state power. The businessman who breaks a contract, the newspaper editor who prints a libelous story, the bus owner who fails to keep his equipment under repair resulting in the injury of a passenger—all may be sued in civil court, and any judgment obtained will be enforced by the state.

From the moralist's point of view, the use of violence by the state in enforcement of law is therefore justifiable because it is necessary to fulfill the function of the state. As we have noted, state violence is no more good in itself than individual violence exerted in defense of a personal right. It is at best an indispensable but regrettable means to a good end, the only alternative to the achievement of which is a worse evil than the use of violence. Violence is not something which can be measured out exactly in gram doses, but sound ethics requires that it be applied only in proportion to need. Under a civilized legal system, the amount of compulsion which the state will use, if necessary, to enforce a judgment or a sentence will depend on a common sense evaluation and balancing of the seriousness of the matter involved and the degree of resistance encountered. It obviously will not invoke the death penalty against a negligent driver who smashes into and wrecks a parked car, nor will it order him shot if he fails to pay the damages assessed. In criminal cases, the sentence will depend on the crime and the circumstances under which it was committed.

There is no need here for a lengthy exposition of modern criminological theory and practice. Most students of the subject will agree that punishment motivated by the idea of retribution is something that will in no way help to achieve that common good which is the end of the state. Many likewise will agree that, while fear of punishment will prevent commission of crime in some cases, it certainly cannot be counted on as an effective general preventive of crime, which must be attacked in its social, economic, and personal roots. Imprisonment, therefore, serves primarily the function of putting the criminal in a position where he can no longer engage in anti-social activities, and, under a model system, of providing the means and incentives to eventual reform.[47] Whether the death penalty as the ultimate expression of legalized state violence is a good or bad thing depends entirely on whether it fulfills a useful and necessary function in proportion to the evil involved. We tend to be sympathetic towards the point of view that, in a truly enlightened penal system, capital punishment will be abolished, but are willing to concede that respectable arguments can be made to the contrary.[48] In any case, this specific issue does not involve the general right of the state to use violence under the conditions we have indicated.

If the state can sometimes legitimately use violence against the individual, can the individual or a group of individuals ever use violence legitimately against the state? We cannot live unmolested within a state and yet not observe those principles of conduct prescribed by law which the state enforces. But just as such forced membership in the state does not preclude the right, commonly exercised in the democratic state, to attempt to modify government policy in accordance with our concept of the desirable, under certain conditions men may even

[47] See E. H. Sutherland, *Criminology*, Philadelphia, 1924, especially Chaps. XVII and XVIII; also F. E. Haynes, *Criminology*, New York, 1930, especially Chaps. V, VI and XVI; M. F. Parmelee, *Criminology*, New York, 1926, especially Chaps. XXIII and XXX; R. M. MacIver, *Society, Its Structure and Changes*, pp. 38–40.

[48] For an eloquent statement of the case against capital punishment, see Luigi Sturzo, *op. cit.*, pp. 225 ff.

justifiably rise in armed revolt against a given government. Beginning as an obvious corollary to the fundamental medieval distinction between the true king and the tyrant, this right of rebellion has received extensive analysis in the writings of scholastic political thinkers and moralists. The great majority of them have agreed that when a government becomes a tyranny which operates contrary to the common good, it may be deposed, by violence if necessary, provided that no non-violent means exist to modify the government's policy satisfactorily, that the majority of the people agree that the government is a tyranny, that there is a reasonable prospect of success, and that the evils involved in violent rebellion are not as great as those involved in the continuance of the tyranny.[49]

In his attempt to show that violence is incapable of achieving "large-scale social reform," Mr. Huxley limits his examples to cases of violent revolution against both the social and political order.[50] We can agree with most of what he has to say about the tendency of violence to perpetuate violence; the reign of terror which so often follows the initial overthrow of a government sows the seeds of new hatreds and further violence. Men of good will do not dispute the desirability of peaceful reform whenever possible. But when the conditions stated above are all met, and only when they are all met, there may be a legitimate use of violence in the attempted achievement of reform. It is, of course, possible to argue that in the twentieth century these conditions can never be met, that the forces unleashed by violent revolution are bound to have such widespread and undesirable repercussions as to run counter to the principle of proportionate evil.[51] We can hope that we nationals of a great functioning de-

---

[49] See, for example, Cronin, *op. cit.*, II, 542.
[50] *Ends and Means*, pp. 25 ff.
[51] St. Thomas Aquinas took essentially the same position in the thirteenth century, arguing that the evils produced in the process of removing a

mocracy will never have to face the necessity for a decision on this point.

But we should at least have no illusions about the effectiveness of non-violence in overthrowing tyranny. Mr. Huxley argues that, since the modern police force is equipped with the latest scientific weapons and can strike with ever-increasing speed and precision, any attempt at violent resistance is futile. It is true that every attempt at violent rebellion against the Nazi leaders petered out in a new roundup by the Gestapo, followed by speedy executions or confinement in a concentration camp. The Nazi tyranny fell only after defeat in a great international war. But this enlargement of the state's power of violence like-wise makes less probable the success of those "non-violent methods of massive non-cooperation and civil disobedience" which he advocates.[52] The almost limitless capacity of brutalized men, working in relays, to slaughter non-resisting human be-ings, as illustrated by the Nazi extermination camps, provides an effective answer to the claim that policemen and soldiers will throw away their guns when they encounter not violent re-sistance but men who fall willing victims to their bullets.[53] The average decent human being enforcing what he believes to be the cause of law and order may well waver and refuse to shoot down masses of men who refuse to retaliate. For him it may be true that "non-violent resistance acts as a sort of moral *jiu-jitsu*. The non-violence and good will of the victim act like the lack of physical opposition by the user of the physical *jiu-jitsu*, to cause the attacker to lose his moral balance. He suddenly and unexpectedly loses the moral support which the usual

tyrant by revolt are worse than the tyranny. See *De Regimine Principum*, trans. Gerald B. Phelan, London and New York, 1938, I, vi.

[52] *Op. cit.*, p. 155.

[53] For a description of the way in which non-violent resistance ideally operates, see Krishnalal Shridharani, *op. cit.*, pp. 35 ff.

violent resistance of most victims would render him." [54] But the mentality of the amoral modern exponent of brute force is less complex and little troubled by need for moral support. For him extermination is a job to be done, with sadistic overtones, and the conduct of the victim is irrelevant. Lack of resistance merely facilitates speedy execution.

With its power to obliterate vast numbers of men in a single explosion, violence in our time is too efficient to make nonviolent resistance practicable against those who have no scruples about using it for the purpose of crushing all opposition. In bygone days, the picture of thousands upon thousands of non-resisters voluntarily throwing themselves before aggressors, leaving only the alternative of marching ahead over their dead bodies, might have had some significance. In the face of modern weapons, and even more the remote-controlled atomic weapons of the future, such non-violent resistance loses all relation to reality.

We come now to the question of violent conflict between states as it expresses itself in the institution of war. Here again the ethical principles are quite clear. Although it involves a much more complex set of circumstances than individual self-defense, war can likewise be justified only as a case of an *indirect voluntary* act. Traditional moral teaching has consistently admitted the theoretical possibility of a just war, and during the past two decades there has been a revived discussion of the conditions each of which must be met to make a war just.[55] Neo-

---

[54] Richard B. Gregg, *The Power of Non-Violence*, Philadelphia, 1934, p. 43.
[55] See for example F. Stratmann, *The Church and War*, London, 1928; Luigi Sturzo, *The International Community and the Right of War*, New York, 1930; *The Ethics of War*, Report of the Ethics Committee of the Catholic Association for International Peace, Washington, 1932; F. Gigon, *The Ethics of Peace and War*, London, 1935; J. Eppstein, *The Catholic*

scholastic writers generally agree that these necessary conditions are: (1) war must be undertaken only in vindication of a strict right; (2) the evil rising out of the deprivation of this right must be proportionate to the evil which will be caused by the war; (3) recourse to war must be a last resort when all non-violent means have been tried and have failed; (4) the state entering upon war must have a reasonable probability of victory; (5) war must be declared by the public authority of the state; (6) the statesmen who make the decision for war must be motivated by the right intention, which is to achieve the vindication of a deprived right; and (7) the actual conduct of the war must be in conformity with ethical principles.[56]

In pre-World War II days, a respectable body of opinion had questioned the possibility of a just war under modern conditions, stressing particularly the question of proportionate evil and the intrinsically immoral methods of twentieth century warfare.[57] But the sweep, the terror and the utter viciousness of the Nazi and Japanese aggression, as well as the endless implications for evil of their victory, permitted men of principle to equate participation in the war with good conscience by balancing tremendous evil against even more tremendous evil. Now that the dread possibilities of atomic fission haunt the minds of men, the problem of war has become almost identical with the problem of human survival. Some will argue that the awful and still largely unknown destructive capacity of this new instrument of power *ipso facto* puts the institution of war beyond

---

Tradition of the Law of Nations, Washington, 1935; E. I. Watkin, *Men and Tendencies*, London, 1937, pp. 290 ff.; G. Vann, *Morality and War*, London, 1939; A. C. F. Beales, *The Catholic Church and International Order*, New York, 1941; John K. Ryan, "Unlimited War and Traditional Morality," *Modern Schoolman*, XXII (1945), 24–32.

[56] *The Ethics of War*, pp. 21 ff.

[57] This was substantially the view taken by Stratmann, Watkin and Vann who are cited in note 55 above.

possibility of justification, while others will prefer to dwell on the almost boundless potentialities for tyranny that the atomic bomb can place in the hands of evil men. On the organizational level, some will claim the immediate necessity for a world government, while others will feel that the better part of wisdom is to build on the possible and that to leave no alternative to what they consider the unobtainable is to invite despair.

In any case, we can say with certainty that no man guided by sound moral principles will provoke or want war. If all the leaders of men strongly desire and work for the elimination of war as a primary ethical requisite, then lasting peace will come to the world. Individual acts of violence we shall always have with us, but the development of war as an institution has reached the point where even the amazing recuperative powers of mankind can no longer keep pace with the destructiveness of new techniques of violence. Let us hope that the organized conscience of the world can prevail, and that the active pursuit of peace by statesmen of good will does not fail because of evil design and disregard for moral values on the part of others. For the disastrous consequences of that failure cannot be measured.

In criticizing doctrines of absolute non-violence and in discussing the principles underlying the legitimate function of violence, we may perhaps unwittingly have given the impression that violence plays a more positive role than it actually does. It is important to have a clear understanding of why violence may be necessary and when it is permissible, but it is also important to know the essential limitations of violence. Violent compulsion is never a good thing; at best, under the conditions which make its use allowable, it involves no moral evil on the part of the user. But its use always involves some privation of a due good which, as the metaphysicians say, is what constitutes evil in the ontological order.[58] From the ontological point of view, the situation of an imprisoned criminal is just as evil as that of a man stranded on a desert island after a shipwreck, since both suffer from a privation of freedom which is a due good of humans. Violence against others, moreover, always involves evil, or attempted evil, in the actual physical order. It may have as objective, and result in, the death of individuals, in their permanent maiming, in their temporary wounding, or perhaps merely in their immediate discomfort or restriction of movement—all of which are physical evils, some serious, some less serious. Only to prevent otherwise inevitable greater evil, physical or moral, in a case of conflict of rights, is the use of violence at all justifiable.

Violence can compel and it can destroy. Hence it can protect right against counterviolence. But its function is essentially negative and non-creative. We can build nothing on violence as such. With it we can only clear away the debris, the obstacles to building; and acts of non-violence must follow if anything positive is to be achieved. "Force saves us only from itself. Men praise the sword because it gives them victory over the sword." [59]

Violence can kill but it cannot convince. It cannot force the assent of free human wills. Because its effect is purely physical and external, leaving the sources and motives of volition untouched, it can never provide finality except through extermination or irreparable injury. Violence against men is always a blow at liberty, and even the violence of legitimate authority suffers from the imperfection of being at best only the lesser of two evils. The continuing discussion in our time of the great problem of authority versus liberty, which is the subject of the chapter that follows, bears eloquent testimony to the del-

---

[58] *Malum est privatio boni debiti.* See St. Thomas Aquinas, *Summa Theologica*, I, 49, 1c; also P. Coffey, *Ontology*, pp. 182 ff.
[59] R. M. MacIver, *op. cit.*, p. 228.

icacy of the margin between justifiable and unjustifiable violence.

In an ideal order of society there would be no need for violence. Each individual would do his duty, and the governing of men would consist solely in the organization and direction of common projects for the general welfare. This would not be the stateless Utopia of the anarchists, but a state based on happy integration and willing cooperation. We are obviously far from such an ideal, and perhaps the best we can hope for is a minimization of conflict through the observance, by as many individuals as possible, of those ethical principles which prohibit the assertion of selfish interests to the detriment of the superior rights of others. The greater the triumph of justice and charity, the closer we can approach universal non-violence. Lacking justice and charity, men and governments will continue to abuse, and in turn fall prey to, the power of violence.

VII

The Power of Authority
and Liberty

ANY DISCUSSION of the correct ordering of power must involve the age-old problem of authority versus liberty. The values which determine how much liberty is desirable and how much compulsion should be exercised by authority under a given set of circumstances are of primary importance in politico-ethical theory. In fact, from one point of view, the problem of power may be considered as largely one of finding the most satisfactory relationship between authority and liberty: the liberty of the individual and the authority of the state, and the liberty of the state and the authority of the international organization of society.

Authority is one of those key-words much used and much abused. Some identify it with rightful power, the right to command. But such a restricted use of the broad term unfortunately does not find general acceptance, and in practice the concept of authority is likely to become mixed up with the concept of power so that the possessor of power is likewise automatically thought of as the possessor of authority. It seems desirable to limit the extension of the term with a modifying adjective in order more clearly to exclude from its scope the unrightful possessors of power, the tyrants, the dictators by terror, who in their time and place do have authority in the popular sense. We may therefore identify rightful power with *legitimate authority*, a term which itself lacks complete precision but which, prescinded from any dynastic connotations, expresses a concept basic to the question of the ethical exercise of power.

Legitimate political authority is a necessary aspect of the functional view of the state which gives to it, as a matter of right, all those powers necessary to carry out its function. In other words, legitimate political authority derives from the right of the state to take action necessary to the general welfare which cannot satisfactorily be achieved by the action of individuals, social groups, or other associations. It involves, of course, not merely the right to use power but the actual possession of power to use; and some may be tempted to say that it is just another term for what is commonly known as sovereignty. And so it may be if we define the latter in terms of right. A vast literature has, however, accumulated on the meaning of sovereignty. The term is usually related to the possession of power, and writers have defined it on various levels of activity as: "the supreme legal, political and physical power of the State to do everything that the State has a moral right to do"; [1] "the will of the nation organized in the state"; [2] "the original, absolute, unlimited power over the individual subject and over all associations of subject"; [3] "that characteristic of the state in virtue of which it cannot legally be bound except by its own will, or limited by any other power than itself"; [4] or the attribute of a "determinate human superior not in a habit of obedience to a like superior" who receives "habitual obedience from the bulk of

[1] John A. Ryan and Francis J. Boland, *Catholic Principles of Politics*, New York, 1940, p. 50.
[2] L. Duguit, *Traité de droit constitutionnel*, Paris, 1911, I, 113.
[3] John W. Burgess, *Political Science and Comparative Constitutional Law*, New York, 1890, p. 52.
[4] Georg Jellinek, *Recht des modernen Staates*, Berlin, 1900, p. 421.

a given society," and whose command is law not subject to any restraint.[5]

The locus of sovereignty in actual practice will obviously depend on how we define it and on the type of state we have in mind; but the doctrine of unlimited state sovereignty, even as a legal fiction, is always a dangerous one. Nor does a rather illogical attempt to limit its application to within the state in order to "save" international law strengthen the doctrine.[6] For if sovereignty is not bound to observe restraint against individuals, there is no higher standard by which it need, as a matter of duty, observe external restraint. It is true that an operating state cannot permit individuals within it to deviate from conduct prescribed by law as necessary to the common good, and must normally be allowed the right of ultimate decision in matters involving the common good. But this power must be strictly qualified in terms of function. The concept of absolute state sovereignty has been ably criticized by many others,[7] and we can only agree that it has no place in a sound and realistic theory of politics.

[5] John Austin, *Lectures on Jurisprudence*, Campbell's 5th ed., London, 1911, Lecture VI.
[6] See James W. Garner, *Political Science and Government*, New York, 1935, pp. 186 ff.
[7] See for example, E. M. Borchard, "Political Theory and International Law," and F. W. Coker, "Pluralistic Theories and the Attack upon State Sovereignty," in Merriam, Barnes and others, *A History of Political Theories: Recent Times*, New York, 1924; L. Duguit, *Etudes de droit publique*, Paris, 1901, Introduction and Chap. I; Harold Laski, *Grammar of Politics*, London, 1925, p. 64 *passim; The Foundation of Sovereignty and Other Essays*, New York, 1921, *passim;* A. D. Lindsay, *The Modern Democratic State*, Oxford, 1943, Vol. I, Chap. IX; R. M. MacIver, *The Modern State*, pp. 467 ff.; Charles M. McIlwain, "A Fragment of Sovereignty," *Political Science Quarterly*, XLVIII (1933), 94–106; Nathaniel Micklem, *The Theology of Politics*, London, 1941, pp. 120 ff., John A. Ryan and Francis J. Boland, *Catholic Principles of Politics*, Chaps. IV and V,

THE NATURE OF LEGITIMATE AUTHORITY

Legitimate political authority, therefore, is a limited authority, and it is measured by the requirements of the common good. The fact that a government misuses its power in a single instance, or in a number of instances, does not, of course, invalidate its basic claim to continuing general authority, provided that abuse of power does not become so chronic as to make its replacement essential to the common good. This common good would not be served by a perpetual somersault of statesmen in and out of office; there must be an element of constancy and predictability in government, and sufficient opportunity for the execution of formulated policy. In the democratic state, the electoral process provides a means for the orderly replacement of policy-makers at reasonable intervals; but the constitutional framework and essential structure of the government remain from administration to administration.

We have used the word legitimate in describing the ethically sanctioned authority of an operating government, but the concept of legitimacy has been given still another meaning which is not irrelevant to this inquiry. To the late Professor Guglielmo Ferrero "a government is . . . legitimate if the power is confined or exercised according to principles and rules accepted without discussion by those who must obey," [8] and "a principle of legitimacy is never isolated . . . it is always in harmony with the customs, the culture, the science, the religion, the economic interests of an age." [9] Such legitimacy is desirable because with it comes relief from that fear of the people by government which leads to the continual excesses of tyranny within the state and a policy of aggression against

[8] *The Principles of Power*, New York, 1942, p. 135.
[9] *Ibid.*, p. 144.

other states.[10] Despite accusations to the contrary, Professor Ferrero's idea of legitimacy differs radically from that of Metternich, and his conclusion is that the legitimate government of the future must be based on the principle of democracy. Some may feel that a good point has been belabored by having had two books written about it. But the point is an important one. Stability based on general acceptance by the people of the constitution under which a government rules is certainly a desirable achievement, and provides an indispensable foundation for the proper functioning of public authority in the common good. Indeed, it seems impossible, in the long run, that the authority of a government can be ethically justified unless it is popularly accepted.

We have said that political authority, in the abstract, derives from the necessity for such authority in the achievement of the state's purpose. But political authority in the concrete always inheres in an operating government of men which does not possess legitimate authority merely because it possesses power. The justification of political authority, therefore, has two aspects—the justification of governmental authority in general, and the justification of such authority in a particular government.

The traditional scholastic doctrine, taught by the great majority of moralists and jurists for over seven hundred years and finding its most complete expression in the two great sixteenth century writers, Cardinal Bellarmine and Francisco Suárez, is that the immediate source of legitimate political authority is

[10] The discovery of a basis for lasting peace and order through the amelioration of this fear is the primary purpose of Professor Ferrero's book cited above, as well as of his earlier *The Reconstruction of Europe*, New York, 1941. See also Ferdinand A. Hermens, *The Tyrants' War and the Peoples' Peace*, Chicago, 1944, Chap. VI, especially pp. 143 ff. for an acute discussion of the role of fear in tyrannical agression.

the people of a community, who have the right to determine under what form of government they shall live.[11] In the words of our Declaration of Independence, "governments derive their just powers from the consent of the governed." During the nineteenth century, one group of neo-scholastics developed a so-called "prior right theory" of the origin of legitimate political authority in the concrete, which stipulated that such authority proceeded directly from God to the rulers of states; [12] but this theory rapidly lost influence and nearly all neo-scholastics in our day adhere to the traditional position.[13] It need hardly be pointed out that those who thus recognize the people's mediate role in the establishment and maintenance of legitimate political authority are far from saying that all authority begins and ends with the people. Nothing begins with the people unless popular consent is a value, and such a value is not born in a vacuum. Its existence and validity depends on the soundness of the general scheme of values of which it is a part. The mistake of Rousseau and the contractualists was to suppose that a state could obtain through the mere consent of individuals any authority, beyond that which possession of dominant power

[11] See Robert Bellarmine, *De Laicis*, trans. Kathleen E. Murphy, New York, 1928, especially Chap. VI; Francisco Suárez, *De Legibus*, III, cap ii, and *Defensio Fidei*, *Catholicae*, III, ii; St. Thomas Aquinas, *Summa Theologica*, II–II, 92, 2.

See also James Bryce, *Studies in History and Jurisprudence*, New York, 1901, p. 529; R. W. and A. J. Carlyle, *A History of Medieval Political Theory in the West*, 6 vols., London and New York, 1903–1936, III, 153; Otto Gierke, *Political Theories of the Middle Age*, trans. F. W. Maitland, Cambridge, 1900, pp. 38 ff.; Luigi Sturzo, *Inner Laws of Society*, New York, 1944, pp. 161 ff.

[12] The most influential work espousing this point of view was Taparelli's *Théorique de droit naturel*, Tournai, 1875. See also Michael J. Cronin, *The Science of Ethics*, 2 vols., New York, 1920, II, especially 499 ff.; and Theodore Meyer, *Institutiones Juris Naturalis*, 2 vols., St. Louis, 1906, II, 434 ff.

[13] See John A. Ryan and Francis J. Boland, *op. cit.*, pp. 72 ff.

could give it, outside the context of a specific ethical system of rights and duties.[14] All legitimate authority must have a moral basis; all authority which does not have a moral basis has no ultimate sanction other than brute force.

Depending upon the institutions which exist in a specific state, the consent of the governed may express itself in various ways, sometimes only in mere acquiescence to the established order of rule. In the last sense, it is equivalent to that general will for the continuance of the fundamental associational framework and law which underlies every operating state.[15] The consent theory is concerned with the immediate source of legitimate political authority, which can presumably be possessed by a monarchy, an oligarchy or a democracy, and not with the best form of government as such. But there can be little doubt that its implications favor the democratic state as providing the best means for the expression of popular consent. We believe it possible to establish, in the abstract, that democracy is the best form of a government,[16] and, given a certain level of political consciousness and capacity, that it is also the best form of government in the concrete. We are thinking here not only of sheer efficiency or material accomplishment—in which the dictator may well excel in the short run—but also in terms of

[14] See above, pp. 39–40; also Yves de la Briere, "The Origin of Political Power," *Modern Schoolman*, XII (1935), 53.

[15] See above, pp. 43–44.

[16] For an exhaustive discussion of various theoretical aspects of the question, leading to the conclusion that on moral grounds democracy is the best form of government, see Mortimer J. Adler and Walter Farrell, O.P., "The Theory of Democracy," *The Thomist*, III (1941), pp. 397–449, 588–652; IV (1942), pp. 121–181, 286–354, 446–522, 692–761; VI (1943), pp. 49–118, 251–277, 367–407; VII (1944), pp. 80–131. See also Mortimer Adler, "The Demonstration of Democracy," *Proceedings of the American Catholic Philosophical Society*, XV (1939), 122–165; "The Demonstrability of Democracy," *The New Scholasticism*, XV (1941), 162–168; Walter Farrell, O.P., "The Fate of Representative Government," *The Thomist*, II (1940), 175–207.

those other criteria which friends of democracy have tradi-
tionally used in its defense.[17] Not least of these is the tendency
of democratic government to make for less abuse of power, less
infringement of desirable liberty than any other form of government. Lord Acton's famous dictum that "Power tends to corrupt and absolute power corrupts absolutely" expresses too un-
conditionally a psychological phenomenon which history has
only too often confirmed. No matter how well-intentioned he
may be, the monarch or dictator ruling with legally unrestrained
power finds the way of coercion and force easier than the
way of persuasion and compromise, and almost inevitably follows the former. A habit of violence grows, and in the opposition there is a progressive development of antipathy, hatred,
and resistance, which can only be suppressed by more violence.
And thus good intentions are forgotten amid the exigencies of
maintaining that absolute power which was originally considered
essential to the achievement of those intentions. When the monarch or dictator with absolute power lacks even good intentions,
when lust for power, pomp, and glory become a dominating
motive, and disregard for the ruled habitual, corruption into
sheer tyranny is speedy and unmitigated.[18]

Some have claimed that democracy makes for war rather than
peace, citing mainly the example of the governments of the
French Revolutionary period [19]—which were, of course, far
from democratic in actual practice. But the fact is, as Clarence

[17] See, for example, John Stuart Mill, *Representative Government*, London, 1861; James Bryce, *Modern Democracies*, 2 vols., New York, 1921, I,
150 ff., II *passim*; A. D. Lindsay, *The Modern Democratic State*, Oxford,
1943, Vol. I, Chap. XI.
[18] Obviously we do not refer here to the legally restrained constitutional
monarch who may very well fit into the institutional framework of a
democratic state.
[19] See Hoffman Nickerson, *The Armed Horde, 1793–1939: a Study of the
Rise, Survival and Decline of the Mass Army*, New York, 1940, *passim*;
also his *Can We Limit War?* New York, 1934.

Streit has pointed out, that of fifteen democratic countries still existing in 1938, no two had fought each other since 1830.[20] No one familiar with the dynamics of twentieth century democracy will for one moment concede that the tendency of popular rule is towards war. In no democractic country prior to World War II was there a general desire for war or a governmental policy designed to bring it about. When it came, there was no joy among the free peoples but only horror at the impending tragedy into which power-lustful men were plunging the world. That they could rise to superb heights of organization and achievement under stress of dire necessity was a tribute to their inner resources and basic strength, but at no time did devotion to a cause ever threaten to develop into liking for war as an institution.

We have quoted Lord Acton with qualified approval about the corrupting effects of power, but not with the intention of denying to legitimate political authority that power which it needs to achieve its purpose. If it is true that absolute power tends to corrupt absolutely, it is likewise true that the farther power is from being absolute, the more restrained it is by custom, by legal safeguards, by the whole structure of democratic institutions which the policy-makers of a given government recognize and abide by, the fewer and less pronounced will be its corrupting effects. There must be power in the democratic state, especially today when the complexities of twentieth century civilization have so tremendously enlarged the sphere of necessary government action. We may fear power, but we cannot deny it to the state if the common good requires action that only government can effectively take. But if our democratic institutions and our will to preserve basic liberties are strong, we may

[20] *Union Now*, New York, 1938, p. 91.

well trust that strong, decisive and capable government will not inevitably lead to the abuse of power.

THE NATURE OF LIBERTY

All abuse of power involves a deprivation of liberty, yet the deprivation of liberty may become a valid and necessary function of power. Under the present organization of society, the power of authority is the primary enemy of liberty, yet it may also be its tried and true friend. This paradoxical relationship between authority and liberty is a delicate one, and the balance can easily be upset. Clear concepts are essential if discussion of the problem is not to end with undue assertion of either one or the other. Unfortunately, the term liberty is highly susceptible to unclear and misleading definition, and many commentators succeed merely in confusing the issue by identifying liberty with various other concepts, modes, or conditions which, no matter how closely related they may be, involve different angles of approach and evaluation. Dr. Dorothy Fosdick has critically analyzed many of these meanings in her useful book *What Is Liberty?* [21] and has argued for what she calls the "literal meaning" of the term. Liberty so conceived is nothing more than "the lack of restraint not merely on what men may care to do at the moment but on what they may care to do." It "involves the continued existence of unclosed possibilities of choice even after one has been taken, allowing a person to continue to do what he wants even if he changes his mind." [22]

We can entirely agree that this concept of liberty as basically absence of restraint is a necessary starting point for any satis-

[21] New York, 1939. As a former student of Professor R. M. MacIver at Columbia University, Dr. Fosdick has amplified the germinal ideas on liberty contained in his lectures and writings.
[22] *Ibid.*, p. 11.

factory discussion of the subject. When men begin by talking about it as an essential condition or a way of life or a process of fulfillment, the path is soon open to the abuse of liberty in the name of liberty. The old expression, "Liberty is not license," is a negative way of saying that a morally acceptable use of liberty should involve the choice of right action. The fact remains, however, that the absence of restraint on licentious or evil conduct is a definite liberty; in a given context it may very well be an undesirable liberty which should be restrained, but not because it is not a liberty. Throughout the centuries the word has acquired so many appealing historical and literary associations that men are reluctant to admit that what they feel to be necessary or desirable action can be contrary to liberty in any way. Hence they will try to distinguish "true" liberty from "false" liberty, or to claim that "real" liberty cannot exist without the presence of certain conditions. No one will deny that more liberties, or a greater degree of specific kinds of liberty, may be present in one type of society than in another; but the most libertarian society involves the suppression of certain liberties, and the most authoritarian society the greater assertion of certain other liberties. Nazi Germany gave more liberty to the ruling party and its leaders than they could possibly have had in a democratic state.

But having said this much, we really have not come very far. Mere absence of restraint is no value in itself, nor can liberty be measured in terms of a strict quantitative formula which makes the total amount of liberty inversely proportional to the total amount of restraint. Those who, like Herbert Spencer, assume both of these points in the affirmative have logically ended in the espousal of anarchy.[23] Absence of restraint in the various

[23] See *ibid.*, pp. 132 ff., for pertinent examples. See also Ernest Barker, *Political Thought in England from Herbert Spencer to the Present Day,*

fields of human activity must be qualitatively evaluated in relation to the effects which specific liberties have on institutions and individuals. Such evaluation presupposes a system of values which in turn must derive from a coherent basic philosophy.

From one point of view, absence of restraint is something purely external and objective; it is either a fact or it is not. But the whole concept of liberty is meaningless unless it also involves a certain capacity in the subjects of liberty, the human beings who are not restrained. It is not merely a question of their feeling free, although that should be a concomitant of the full fact of freedom, but of their actually having freedom of choice between alternatives. Men sometimes speak of captured animals escaping into liberty; and some would perhaps claim that the liberty of the escaped lion and the liberty of the citizen of a democratic state are essentially the same, in that both consist solely of freedom from external restraint on those actions towards which internal non-voluntary causes (such as instinct, behavioristic reaction to environment or mechanistic activity of the brain) inexorably impel. But what an illusion is liberty if internal restraint is never absent, if authority merely does not prevent people from doing what they cannot help doing, regardless of reasoning, argument or motive! Political theory cannot ignore the problem of free will; any adequate discussion of liberty must deal with its psychology. On the political level, the fact of free will must be an integral part of any effective argument against those who would deny the role of liberty in the achievement of that common good which is the end of the state.

We can agree in a loose sense with Dr. Fosdick that "claims for liberty spring from the desire of men to give expression

London and New York, 1924, Chap. IV, for an illuminating discussion of Spencer's political writings.

to their individuality," that "liberty is effective in releasing the individuality of men," and that "there is ground for believing that some liberties are more essential than others as *conditions for releasing the actual individuality of men.*" [24] But without a definite philosophy of human nature and value in terms of which the "actual individuality of man" may be stated and the release of man's individuality proved to be a good thing, such generalizations mean little. Many writers on the subject simply jump from them to a discussion of specific or "fundamental" liberties, assuming a whole theory of human nature with scarcely a reference to it. While this neglect of a basic issue might not leave a serious hiatus in an age of common agreement upon essentials, it can scarcely suffice in a twentieth century of conflicting ideologies and values many of which involve a view of human nature that makes the cause of liberty a sham and a delusion.

Who then is the ideally free man? The designation obviously cannot be restricted to one enjoying complete freedom both from internal and external restraint, for such a person does not and cannot exist on this earth. Apart from the restraints of society, the very limitations of his physical nature imposes upon each man a whole series of restraints. The most a person can hope for is the attainment of the maximum amount of liberty in every sphere of activity consistent with his capacities. To some, perhaps, the gamboling savage pictured by certain romantics, free from all the inhibitions of organized society and its codes, living without care off a friendly nature, might seem best to fit the description of free man; but apart from the anthropological falsity of this factitious conception of the primitive, it is absurd to make ignorance and lack of development a pre-

[24] *Op. cit.,* pp. 154, 157. The italics are Dr. Fosdick's own. A better word than "individuality" would be "personality."

requisite of freedom. The primitive does enjoy certain liberties which are denied to men in a more complex society, but these are on a lower level of experience than those liberties which life in an advanced social and intellectual milieu alone can provide. On the other extreme, some may feel that the truly free man is the "emancipated" modern, the *bon vivant* and free-thinker, who partakes of all the benefits of twentieth century civilization but defies the codes and conventions of church and society, who lives where he pleases, loves whom he pleases, eats and drinks what he pleases, and generally does as he pleases, maintaining only those minimum alimony payments and observances of regulation necessary to keep himself out of jail. It is true that such a person possesses many liberties, some of which may be highly desirable in terms of strictest morality. Others of his liberties will be highly undesirable in such terms, and continued breach of all the rules of personal ethics that one can get away with is likely to backfire. Many, for example, have discovered from sad experience that liberty to disregard the dictates of moderation in eating and drinking loses its attractiveness with the onset of chronic indigestion and pink elephants. Unrestrained defiance of those established rules of conduct grounded in the functional necessities of human nature and formulated through the long experience of many generations of men does not lead to maximum enjoyment of freedom. The end result may well be slavery to a single vicious habit.

Neo-scholastic writers on the subject have sometimes fallen into the confusion of identifying liberty with liberties desirable in terms of the moral code. Even so acutely careful a thinker as Jacques Maritain has, in his *Freedom in the Modern World*,[25] left himself open to this charge through a failure to make it sufficiently clear at the outset that he is discussing primarily the

[25] Trans. Richard O'Sullivan, London, 1935, Part I.

relation of liberty to free will; [26] although a broader reading of his works would show that he is fully aware of the fact that, externally considered, liberty is absence of restraint.[27] On the other hand, neo-scholastics have never fallen into the opposite confusion of imagining that mere absence of restraint can have any real significance, or its desirability be determined, except in relation to specific persons who are not being restrained. Some men have more liberties than others. Some feel that they are free when they are actually constrained in many essentials. Others feel oppressed even though they have many liberties. The ideally free man both feels free and is free. He enjoys all of those external absences of restraint which may serve a functional purpose in the highest development of the human person. His knowledge of the world and of himself, his control of those passions and habits which vitiate the power of voluntary decision, are so integrated and so consistent as to insure maximum freedom of choice in any given situation.

Freedom of choice does not involve, as many determinists imagine, a complete lack of positive determination, an operation of a mysterious faculty in a mental grab bag. Nor is it an expression of the totality of the psychical organism in the sense of Henri Bergson.[28] According to the traditional conception, the will is an appetite rooted in the intellect; its ultimate object is absolute good; and its action is essentially undetermined when there is an indetermination of the judgment regarding a choice of action.[29] In the act of free choice, as Cajetan has expressed it,

[26] See Dorothy Fosdick, *op. cit.*, pp. 63–65.
[27] See his *Scholasticism and Politics*, trans. and ed. by Mortimer Adler, New York, 1940, Chap. V; also his *True Humanism*, New York, 1938, pp. 171 ff.
[28] See his *Time and Free Will*, trans. F. L. Pogson, London, 1910, pp. 165 ff.
[29] See St. Thomas Aquinas, *Summa Theologica*, I, 82; I, 83, for a classic statement. See also Jacques Maritain, *Scholasticism and Politics*, pp. 119 ff. and *Freedom in the Modern World*, pp. 3 ff.; J. Lindworsky, *Theoretical*

the will bends the judgment in the direction it desires.[30] This does not mean that men always act the way they want to and then rationalize to prove they acted rightly, but that the will dominates the indeterminate judgment by "an act which rises from the depths of personality." [31] The indeterminate judgment is not essentially one of good versus evil—although that may well be the most important issue—but of to act or not to act, of to act in this way or in that way.[32] There must always be a choice of internal alternatives, even though one of these is merely the possibility of not willing to do that which one is forced to do. Without such alternatives, there is no freedom of choice.

Needless to say, the question of free will is one of considerable complexity to which some of the greatest minds of history have devoted much thought and analysis. Modern science has shown that many human acts derive their essential impetus from various non-rational and non-volitional factors, both psychological and physiological; but progressively fewer will claim that its findings leave no room for the operation of free choice in the normal reasonably balanced individual. Absolute determinism is not only opposed to the practical experience and common sense conviction of the majority of the human race but is unsubstantiated by any empirical evidence.[33] Although the

---

Psychology, trans. H. R. DeSilva, St. Louis, 1932, pp. 101-108 and *Der Wille*, Leipzig, 1923, pp. 280 ff.; Michael Maher, *Psychology*, 9th ed., New York, 1926, Chap. XIX; Desiré Mercier, *A Manual of Scholastic Philosophy*, 2d ed., trans. T. L. and S. A. Parker, St. Louis, 1919, I, 263-277; Yves R. Simon, "Liberty and Authority," *Proceedings of the American Catholic Philosophical Association*, XVI (1940), 86-114; J. de la Vaissière, *Elements of Experimental Psychology*, trans. S. A. Raemers, St. Louis, 1926, Chap. VIII.

[30] Cited by Maritain in *Scholasticism and Politics*, p. 129.
[31] *Ibid.*, p. 127.
[32] Called by Aquinas, *liberty of exercise* and *liberty of specification*.
[33] See J. Lindworsky, *op. cit.;* J. de la Vaissière, *op. cit.;* also Vincent Herr, "The Use of Freedom in Everyday Life," and John W. Stafford, "Freedom in Experimental Psychology," both in *Proceedings of the*

rather muddled speculations of certain physicists, who have tried to use the principle of indeterminism as proof of free will, have tended to confuse the issue,[34] there are strong arguments for voluntarism which can stand the most careful scrutiny and criticism. Defenders of liberty need not feel that their cause is based on psychological illusion, nor need they, like Arthur Koestler,[35] take refuge in a double standard of truth which admits free will on the moral level, because without it there can be no morality, but denies it on the scientific level.

The act of intellection and the act of willing are both integrally bound up with the development of the human person. As a man grows in wisdom and knowledge he becomes more free from the bondage of error, hidden motivation, and uncertain analysis. As he freely wills to act in accordance with his functional nature he becomes more free from the restraints of indecision and bad habit, and his nature is perfected. Liberty to thus act is therefore necessary to the perfecting of the person of man; and the whole philosophy of personalism espoused by Jacques Maritain and many neo-scholastics, which has received so much discussion in recent years, is, from one point of view, a justification of liberty in society.[36]

American Catholic Philosophical Association, XVI (1940), 143–148 and 148–154, respectively.

[34] See Henry V. Gill, *Fact and Fiction in Modern Science*, New York, 1944, Chap. VIII.

[35] See his *The Yogi and the Commissar*, New York, 1945, pp. 218 ff.

[36] See Jacques Maritain, *Scholasticism and Politics*, Chap. III; *The Rights of Man and Natural Law*, New York, 1943, pp. 1 ff.; Emmanuel Mounier, *A Personalist Manifesto*, New York, 1938; M. Lamarié, *Essai sur la personne*, Paris, 1936. For a criticism of personalism see Charles de Koninck, *De la primauté du bien commun contre les Personnalistes; le principe de l'ordre nouveau*, Quebec, 1943, and for a specific defense T. Eschmann, "In Defense of Jacques Maritain," *The Modern Schoolman*, XXII (1945), 183–208.

It may be noted that the personalists make a basic distinction between individuality and personality, a distinction which is valid and necessary as

We have said that without *internal* alternatives, even though one alternative is merely the possibility of not willing to do that which one is forced to do, there can be no freedom of choice. But as Don Luigi Sturzo has emphasized, without *external* alternatives it is still possible freely to will to do that to which there is no alternative.[37] If, however, men will to do otherwise, without external alternatives they obviously have no freedom of action, though their wills may be uncrushed and they may continue choosing to do that which they cannot. Men may *feel* free under a tyranny because they possess liberty of internal choice, recognizing and defying as far as possible the constraints which the possession of dominant physical power enables the tyrant to impose. Yet such a situation is at best unsatisfactory. There is little scope for the expression of personal desires and initiative, and weaker men may soon achieve that dubious condition of external liberty where they feel no restraint because they have rationalized themselves into not wanting to do that which they cannot do.

In any state, the direct function of the compulsive power of authority is to eliminate certain external alternatives, and therefore its application always restricts some liberties. The ultimate object may well be the protection of certain other liberties the enjoyment of which is incompatible with the prohibited liberties. But the fact that the liberties of some may destroy the liberties of others in itself provides no criterion of desirable state action, since competitive relationships between individuals usually result in the loss of some liberties by someone. When two men want the same job and one of them gets it, the other is deprived

---

they are defined, but which may seem to involve a somewhat arbitrary arrogation of meaning to these terms. See Jacques Maritain, *The Rights of Man*, pp. 2–3; *Scholasticism and Politics*, pp. 56 ff. But see also Etienne Gilson, *The Spirit of Medieval Philosophy*, New York, 1936, Chap. X, especially p. 202. [37] See his *Inner Laws of Society*, p. 178.

of a specific economic liberty—absence of restraint on his choice of work; yet ordinarily the state would properly not intervene. On the other hand, it is likewise not enough to say that desirable liberties are those which serve a functional purpose in the development of the human person. Supposing an individual chooses to act contrary to his function. Should the state prohibit each such action? Obviously not. But when should authority restrict liberty? The question is one of considerable complexity, yet certain broad governing principles may be stated.

AUTHORITY VERSUS LIBERTY: TRUE OR FALSE ANTITHESIS

The restraints on human activity are legion, and at least in the non-totalitarian state the majority are not imposed directly by state authority but rise out of social, economic, and personal relationships. While liberty must not be identified with means or conditions, it remains a fact that the absence of necessary means or conditions can constitute just as much a restraint on activity as a direct prohibition enforced by superior power. Behind the whole structure of social, economic, and personal relationships protected by law is the authority of the state; and the state will intervene, by force if necessary, whenever violations of that law occur or are apparently threatened.

Liberties are often competitive, not only in the abstract but through the concrete choices of action which men make. There is no essential harmony of interests between the selfish wants of men, as nineteenth century liberals so naively imagined.[38] No special acuteness is required to discern throughout modern society a constant conflict of interests, as those interests are understood by their possessors. The problem, therefore, becomes one of determining which are the most important liberties, the fundamental liberties, which the state should preeminently protect,

[38] See above, pp. 30–33.

or at least not interfere with. Any discussion of "fundamental" liberties is, of course, meaningless except in terms of a system of values under which they are fundamental; and here, as elsewhere in the field of political and social thought, the unrealized implications of a basic philosophy inimical to positive value-judgments can vitiate the best of intentions. Liberty is not an absolute value in itself, and many of the inconsistencies of the liberal position derived from a tendency to view it as such. Specific liberties can only be justified as necessary conditions for the achievement of some permanent value.

The end of legitimate authority, as we have seen, is the common good. This is not a "mere aggregation of particular goods, and is not the peculiar good of a whole which . . . relates only to itself and sacrifices the parts to itself; it is the common good *of the whole and its parts*, a good which integrates particular goods in the whole so far as they are communicable . . . and as it is itself communicable to the parts." [39] Life in society brings to individuals a certain well-being and a possibility of development which they could not have in a non-social form of existence. As Professor MacIver has written, "We can fulfil our nature only in and through society; moreover the nature that is thus fulfilled is itself a social nature." [40] But the common good is no mystical entity with existence or purpose distinct from the individuals who partake of it. It involves the fullest possible development of every person consistent with the fullest possible development of every other person, and hence the furtherance of those liberties which are indispensable to such fullest possible development. The ultimate resort of authority is coercion but its objective should be not to constrain but to liberate. Thus the law of the state may ideally be described as "the pedagogue of

[39] Jacques Maritain, *The Things That Are Not Caesar's*, trans. J. F. Scanlan, London, 1932, p. 139n. The italics are Maritain's.
[40] *Society, Its Structure and Changes*, New York, 1931, p. 20.

liberty," [41] and any state which, in the long run, works counter to the emancipation of human personality is bad and its authority without moral foundation. "In the order of social life, it thus appears that the end of civil life is a common earthly good and a common earthly undertaking, whose *highest values* consist in aiding the human person so that it may free itself from the servitudes of nature and achieve its autonomy in regard to the latter." [42]

Liberation is not, of course, always a primary implication of the common good. Under certain circumstances, such as great disaster or crisis, the common good may well require the temporary subordination of even fundamental liberties to insure the preservation of those general conditions without which such liberties, and perhaps life itself, could not exist. But with the ending of critical danger and the return of peace and social order, the fundamental liberties must again be permitted to assume their constructive role in the perfection of human personality.

There are as many liberties possible in the abstract as there are courses of action which men may want to follow. Within the area of our inquiry, we may find useful as a starting point Don Luigi Sturzo's broad division of the fundamental liberties into *original* liberty, *organic* liberty, *finalistic* liberty, and *formal* liberty.[43] By *original* liberty is meant that basic freedom in the endowment of government with power which men are conceived to have, not in a strict historical or contractualist sense, but in the sense of a primary title to authority and a permanent limit on it. This concept is expressed in the statement that the immediate source of legitimate political authority is the con-

[41] The phrase is Maritain's. See his *True Humanism*, p. 176.
[42] Jacques Maritain, *Scholasticism and Politics*, pp. 136–137.
[43] *Inner Laws of Society*, pp. 161–203.

sent of the governed.[44] *Organic* liberty is defined as "both free initiative in the creation of social organisms adapted to the manifold needs of life, and freedom within these organisms";[45] *finalistic* liberty refers to that freedom consciously to share in the determination of those particular ends of the state which are meant to achieve the general end of the common good.[46] *Formal* liberty is that absence of restraint on the various political, cultural, religious, economic, and social activities of men which is permitted or protected by the power of authority. In the concrete there are obviously a great multitude of specific *formal* liberties.

We have already discussed certain aspects of *original* liberty and *finalistic* liberty, and have expressed preference for a modified "consent theory" of the immediate origin of legitimate political authority, and for democracy as a form of government, which are, respectively, the obverse of these two liberties. The question of *organic* liberty leads us directly into the great debate over pluralism which took place during the first three decades of the twentieth century. In reaction to the prevailing doctrine of unlimited and exclusive state sovereignty, the pluralists argued that sovereignty is divisible among the various associations or groups that make up society, and that the state has neither superior claim to the allegiance of individuals nor the right specifically to regulate the groups which they form and which possess distinct, natural, corporate personalities.[47] The role

[44] *Ibid.*, pp. 164–173.
[45] *Ibid.*, p. 174. "Organizational" might be a better word than "organic" in this connection, since the latter has too many strictly biological connotations and is associated with the discredited organismic theory of the state.
[46] *Ibid.*, pp. 176–178.
[47] See F. W. Coker, "Pluralistic Theories and the Attack upon State Sovereignty," in Merriam, Barnes and Others, *A History of Political Theories: Recent Times*, New York, 1924, for a good summary of pluralis-

of the state is reduced to that of an umpire between conflicting associations.

Now the theory of pluralism is more complex than a bald statement of its essential claim would perhaps make it appear. Many of the pluralists, such as Cole, Penty, Carpenter, and Russell, were also guild Socialists or Syndicalists advocating a radical reform of economic society, and their whole approach has had predominantly economic overtones. Be that as it may, any satisfactory formulation of the modern state's role in society must involve the concept of limited sovereignty, and must take into account the important role of the great associations in meeting the manifold needs of human nature. Liberty of organization, within the limits indicated below, is a primary right; and to imply that the state can legitimately deny that right simply because it is sovereign, without reference to criteria for the proper use of its superior power, is to align oneself logically, if not in intention, with the exponents of totalitarian *Gleichschaltung*. It is true that there must be in society a final political authority with the right to take such action as may be necessary in achievement of its end—the common good; and the refusal of the pluralists to admit this is the primary weakness of their position. But the common good itself requires a maximum liberty of organization in all cases where the end of organization is good. There obviously cannot be liberty of bigger and better organization for racketeers and gunmen, for illicit drug merchants, or for any other purpose specifically contrary to the general welfare.

Liberty of organization is not therefore absolute. While it is

---

tic theory. See also G. D. H. Cole, *Guild Socialism*, London, 1920, Chaps. I and II; J. N. Figgis, *Churches in the Modern State*, London, 1913, *passim;* M. P. Follett, *The New State*, London, 1920, *passim;* Harold J. Laski, *Grammar of Politics*, London, 1925, Chap. VII, and *Problem of Sovereignty*, London, 1917, *passim;* F. W. Maitland, Introduction to *Political Theories of the Middle Ages*, London, 1900.

generally true that the state should regulate the great associations which "have an inner life . . . at least as autonomous as that of the state . . . only in respect of their common external attributes, controlling such universal institutions as contract and property so as to maintain and develop the form of social order within which they must all move" [48]—the history of the Nazi party and of fascist and communist groups in general during the past twenty years has underlined the need for an earlier and more stringent control over the organization of men if such organization is based on ideals and methods clearly contrary to the common good. Just when the state has a right to intervene is not always an easy question to answer in the concrete. There is always the factor of human error and waywardness which can turn an initially innocent or worthy organization into a harmful one, but the state obviously cannot ban merely in anticipation of a trend of policy and action. Only when an organization by announced intention and actual deed becomes a "menace" to the general welfare is there a valid case for specific preventive regulation. The principles involved tend to merge with those applicable to certain of the formal liberties, and our consideration of the latter will help further to clarify the problem of organizational liberty.

The *formal* liberties enjoyed by men have varied from age to age, from culture to culture, from people to people. But sound theory confirmed by experience has come to the recognition that certain formal liberties are necessary in the perfection of personality. In the modern democratic state, the right to designated formal liberties is often written into the basic constitution; or in the case of a largely unwritten consitution, such as England's, more or less the same liberties have gradually been integrated into the body of rights protected by precedent and

[48] R. M. MacIver, *The Modern State*, p. 182.

practice. There are, of course, also a host of "informal" liberties which have no relationship to the juridical organization of society. They require no toleration or protection by the state since they never come into conflict with the power of authority, no matter how tyrannically excerised, nor are they seriously threatened by, or of noticeable inconvenience to, other individuals. A man may part his hair in the middle or on the side as he chooses, and even the modern totalitarian state will not attempt to regulate the location of his part. Life for each of us is full of these little liberties which are secure from forceful external restraint if not always from the high-pressure salesman. While they are desirable enough to the person concerned, no one of them is specifically essential for the fullest development of personality.

While the *formal* liberties may be classified under certain broad categories each representing a primary area of human activity in which certain liberties are ordinarily desirable, they are not hermetically sealed one from the other, but are all part of a vast complex of interacting motivation, cause and effect. Upon analysis, some appear inalienable by basic right, others justifiable merely because of changing circumstance. All-inclusive generalizations about them are apt to mislead, and not the least misleading has been the attempt to divide the *formal* liberties into those which affect only the individual who has them and those which affect others as well. Only the latter, it is then argued, should be subject to regulation. Superficially, this approach seems plausible enough, and there are, as we have noted, many informal liberties which affect only the person who enjoys them to any noticeable extent. But the formal liberties tend to have more extensive ramifications, and the endeavor to immunize any of them from regulation because they affect only their possessor breaks down in the face of a widening chain of causality extending from free activity. Even freedom of thought inasmuch as it expresses itself in speech, writings, or action affects society to some extent; and the Japanese attempt at thought-control cannot be condemned simply on the ground that thought never affects anyone except the thinker.

John Stuart Mill's discussion of liberty in his essay *On Liberty* [49] is largely vitiated by his division of acts into those which belong to the individual and those which belongs to society. His criterion of acts involving "a distinct and assignable obligation to others" for those which do not belong only to the individual has little meaning in view of his failure clearly to define "distinct," "assignable," and above all "obligation." A workable evaluation of the claims of specific liberties against the power of authority entails more than the consideration of who is affected by them. Also important are the kinds of affects which exercise of a liberty may have, as well as the end towards which and the circumstances under which it is exercised; and only in the light of all these determinants can the desirability of a liberty be established or denied.

In discussing the regulation of formal liberties by the power of state authority, it is well to remember that government is not an infallible organ of control. It can and often does make mistakes, erring by excess or lack of zeal, by faulty judgment, and by sheer stupidity. In the hands of wicked men, it can adopt an evil policy animated by bad will and perverse objectives. In the ideal, the state should embody in its legal codes and precedents the collective wisdom and experience of a people, and, resting on the general will for its continued existence, should stand above conflicting groups as the enforcing agency for those conditions which permit the maximum development of personality for the many. In reality, however, a specific govern-

[49] London, 1859.

ment may represent nothing more than a faction, a section of society, which has gained power and seeks to advance solely its own particularistic interests. On the other hand, while the state has no a priori claim to obedience under all circumstances, it does have the right to act within its function. Our entire faith in the necessity of the state involves the assumption that good government and even indifferent government serve the general welfare in enough ways, and are right sufficiently often, to warrant the power which they possess. An imperfect form of equilibrium between the claims of authority and liberty is achieved in the modern democratic state. Not all of the desirable liberties are realizable to the fullest extent because certain necessary conditions do not exist. But attainment of the best possible relationship between authority and liberty remains an ideal of democracy, and this fact is integral to its justification.

THE FORMAL LIBERTIES: THEIR VALUE AND LIMITATION

We may consider the formal liberties from two points of view: (1) the spheres of human activity in which they may exist, such as the cultural, the political, and the economic, and (2) the general ways in which liberties in these various spheres may be exercised, such as by freedom of conscience and thought, freedom of investigation and research, and freedom of expression and teaching. It is desirable to note certain broad principles governing the latter, which apply to all of the specific spheres of activity, before attempting to discuss basic aspects of the cultural, political, and economic liberties as such. Needless to say, in addition to these over-all liberties or modes of exercise, there are liberties distinctive to each sphere. Thus absence of restraint on elections to government office is a form of political liberty, and absence of restraint on sales of property is a form of economic liberty.

Freedom of conscience and thought may at the outset be designated as unsuitable for regulation by the power of authority. Force cannot make a person think a good thing bad or a bad thing good, a true thing false or a false thing true. It can kill or dull by torture, but it cannot win assent from the mind which it has not first brutalized. It cannot even get at the inner thoughts of men. They may mouth lies, make verbal commitments, in order to escape punishment, but there is no real conviction. It is true that a twentieth century tyranny can use the instruments of persuasion provided by modern propaganda methods, and can break down the resistance of weaker men by an interminable barrage of lies and half-truths.[50] Eventually its victims may even be persuaded to welcome restrictions and to favor evil policies instead of resenting them. But it is not essentially force that brings about this change except as it prevents the expression of any distracting or opposing opinions. Attempts at so-called thought-control involve taking their clue from unguarded statements and then punishing the thinker for having "dangerous" thoughts. They do not really control his thought, though they may end it by ending him.

At least until recently, most men of good will would have agreed that freedom of investigation and research should likewise be immune from regulation by the power of authority. What but good could come from the impartial search for truth and the increase of human knowledge? The picture of the mad scientist concocting some fiendish brew of microbes, or some death-dealing ray, aroused fear only among devotees of science

[50] See Amber Blanco White, *The New Propaganda*, London, 1939, especially section I, for an acute analysis of the propaganda methods of the modern dictator. For an interesting discussion of the possible long-run effects of the new propaganda see R. M. MacIver, *Leviathan and the People*, Baton Rouge, La., 1939, pp. 54-55, 135-137.

wonder fiction and the fantasies of H. G. Wells. But the making of the atomic bomb, and the combination of theory, research, technique, and organization which went into its manufacture, has raised serious questions regarding the extent to which freedom of investigation can be permitted in the field of atomic fission. The development of a source of energy with such overwhelming potentialities for either good or evil can obviously not be left to the fortuities of individual whim and preference. On the other hand, any rigid strait-jacketing of research is likely to hinder further progress and discovery. The great scientific advances of the past one hundred and fifty years have been favored by the generally prevailing atmosphere of political nonrestraint over the work of scientists; and it seems clear that freedom of investigation is definitely related to maximum progress within a given field of inquiry.[51]

Can the demands of public safety and of free investigation be harmonized? Most Americans will concede that the situation requires more than purely national approaches, and that, ultimately, some form of effective international control over both the manufacture and use of atomic weapons alone can provide satisfactory guarantee against their abuse. Once such control is instituted, individual scientists will be at liberty to continue their investigations within the general framework of international supervision. Such supervision may well involve the banning of certain types of research; for in the applied sciences, research is not something which can be separated from the actual process of manufacture. Based on a laboratory discovery, an innovation may be planned in a weapon. Designs are drawn up and revised as research continues and eliminates flaws; the

[51] For an eloquent exposition of the view that basic freedom of inquiry is incompatible with the planned state, see John R. Baker, *Science and the Planned State*, New York, 1945.

first model is completed and tested; other flaws develop, which it is the task of further research to eliminate; and finally, after a series of additional tests and improvements based on continuing research, all major defects are eliminated and the new weapon is ready for quantity production.

Absolute claims for freedom of investigation and research are therefore likely to be incompatible with the requirements of the general welfare even under the optimum form of international organization. And this is only common sense. Upon analysis, it becomes clear that there have always been certain desirable limitations on such freedom. After all, it is not in the same category as freedom of conscience and thought. While it may add to the sum total of knowledge, research requires material things upon which it can be exercised; and material things, especially those dealt with in the physical sciences, can do damage to living men. An elementary form of limitation which may be desirable is that of location. Laboratories cannot go up anywhere. Zoning laws will prohibit certain types of construction in certain areas; public authority will scarcely permit a laboratory for experimentation on dangerous explosives or gases to be built in a crowded residential section. And once the laboratory is under operation, safety regulations will ban certain practices to protect the workers.

Apart from this control in the interests of public safety justifiable because the very process of research can be physically dangerous, regulation may also be desirable because of probable or certain abuse of the end product. For some time at least, the Western powers may hesitate to grant Germany and Japan full freedom of investigation and research in methods of warfare and armament manufacture. Few will deny that, given general trust and security, knowledge of this kind could well be dispensed with by all nations. Since it is frequently impossible to ascertain the researcher's motives—whether he (or his sponsor) is animated by anti-social and destructive intentions—regulating authority must generally rely on subject matter as its chief criterion. There are certain types of knowledge and technique which can only be put to bad use if they are put to any use at all. Gestapo research in the art of inflicting torture, of extracting information from hapless victims, was always a vicious activity, one that deserved to be crushed and prohibited any time, anywhere; and we can say the same of any endeavor specifically intended to increase the pain of this world.[52] Research in the technique of counterfeiting currency, if conducted by private individuals, is likely to bring police raids and incur the general wrath of public authority despite protestations that all the inks, presses, and paper involved are only means in a pure quest for knowledge.

Without being obscurantist, we can agree therefore that men are better off without certain knowledge because such knowledge brings only greater power to do harm. Freedom of investigation in this area is not a value and may be a great evil. We can also agree that certain other knowledge with great potentiality for both good and evil may in its acquisition be subject to justifiable regulation in order to prevent disastrous abuse. And finally, we can agree that the search for knowledge—even beneficial knowledge—does not involve the right to use every means for its attainment, that the Nazi use of concentration camp inmates for various mass "experiments" resulting in death to numerous human guinea pigs was a travesty on the scientific attitude.

The field of knowledge is vast, and all that is known today

[52] This obviously does not refer to properly conducted vivisection, which may involve the infliction of pain on animals in the quest for knowledge with which to do good, and ultimately to alleviate a greater amount of pain.

is accessible to no one person. But mankind has just begun to accumulate facts on many subjects and to theorize about them. Freedom to investigate, to acquire knowledge, should be the rule unless the common good demands otherwise. Ordinarily the mere possibility of abuse is not sufficient to warrant regulation unless the magnitude of possible abuse, as in the case of atomic energy, is such as directly to threaten the welfare of the human race or a considerable part of it. If the character of the researcher, his past reputation, make possibility a probability— that is another matter.

In one sense, freedom of expression and teaching is a necessary complement to freedom of investigation and research. Without it, the acquisition of accurate knowledge is difficult, often impossible, and knowledge already possessed tends to become sterile. But there is also a difference in amplitude between the two liberties. Investigation and research imply an earnest intention to get at the truth of things, even if they be bad things, or the quest be impelled by bad motives or end in failure and error. Expression and teaching, on the other hand, need have no connection with the truth at all, even in aspiration. Goebbels at his worst enjoyed the same liberty as the most sincere town hall orator pleading for a worthy cause. Because words and graphic displays can be used to convey gross distortions and pernicious errors, to advocate cruelty and every type of evil, the relation of this liberty to public authority has long been the subject of great debate which in our day is still far from settled.

The general principles are clear, but their application amid the complexities of human behavior is full of difficulty. Like all other liberties, that of expression and teaching has no absolute value. It is but a means to an end and, when the general welfare so demands, it is rightly subject to regulation. But when does the general welfare so demand? The tendency in the nine-teenth century Western world was towards an ever greater latitude in the expression of opinion. Liberal theory was domi-nant with its emphasis on the greatest possible amount of free-dom, and men generally agreed that public authority was ill-qualified to control something the true test of which lay out-side the scope of power. In the twentieth century, there has been a great reversion from this trend; and many states have at-tempted rigid regimentation of expression and teaching as part of a generally repressive and tyrannical policy—a development underlining the importance of free expression and teaching in the preservation of our cultural heritage and its values which, in the past, some have been tempted to think were more threat-ened by "excess" of liberty.

Freedom of expression and teaching is a valuable liberty, some-thing to be cherished and defended. But certainly not because of the relativist claim that, since we can never be sure of the truth, no one has any right to impose one point of view on an-other. That sort of argument can quickly be turned around to justify the extinction of the formal liberties. In a completely relativist world, they mean nothing, since they lead to nothing except objectives which have only illusory value. The repudia-tion of all certitude invites the conclusion that, if truth and value do not make right, then might makes it very well.

Nor is it enough to fall back on "our deep-seated conviction of the excellence of freedom," assuming that it is impossible "to show either by practical test or by rigorous reasoning the supe-riority of liberty over constraint." [53] If we cannot show the nor-

[53] Edward P. Cheyney, "Observations and Generalizations," in Symposium on "Freedom of Inquiry and Expression," *Annals of the American Acad-emy of Political and Social Science*, CC (1938), 275. This is likewise what the argument of John P. Plamenatz boils down to in his *Consent, Free-dom and Political Obligation*, Oxford, 1938, p. 143.

mal superiority of liberty by rigorous reasoning in terms of logically established values, then we had better give up trying to defend liberty at all. Freedom of expression and teaching may require regulation under certain circumstances, but not because coercion is ever a higher value in itself than liberty. The free act towards a good end is always better than a compulsory act towards a good end, even though both may achieve the same result. A free expression of belief has significance; a forced expression of supposed belief means nothing, and compounds misuse of power with a lie.

A primary value of freedom of expression and teaching lies in its direct relationship to the preservation of men's rights in the various other areas of liberty. Without it, most of the important liberties are either impossible or abortive. Even freedom of conscience and thought is likely to wear thin in the protracted absence of ability to express one's views. Freedom of research and investigation without freedom to impart the results of research, or to draw on the results of previous work in the same field, would be largely meaningless; and freedom to inform, to discuss, to argue, and to convince is just as obviously a necessary condition to the efficacious exercise of the various cultural, political, and economic liberties.

Moreover, the highest development of men's personalities and creative faculties would seem to be linked to a generally prevailing atmosphere of free discussion. Only the rare individual can rise above the stagnation inevitably found in a society of rigidly controlled expression and teaching. Unless men can freely propound, receive, examine, compare, accept or reject the opinions and theories of other men, progress towards better living and fuller development of personality is scarcely possible. As Louis le Fevre has pointed out, "The most unfortunate aspect of intellectual stagnation is that it tends to perpetuate itself. Where the general level of mental activity is low, the stimulation of contact with superior minds is lacking. The absence of the clash of ideas . . . is an immense handicap." [54] While truth is not relative, the state of knowledge in a given field may well be far from accurate or complete. It is likely to remain that way unless men can compare notes on a broad scale, can pool their individual knowledge through the various existing media of communication, and can inspire in others through their teaching the same thirst for knowledge so that they will continue the quest.

This, in substance, is the sound part of the traditional liberal argument for freedom of expression and teaching, the classic statement of which is found in John Stuart Mill's essay *On Liberty* and his essay *On Social Freedom*. It is an argument with which all men of good will should agree. Anyone who imagines, for example, as some apparently do, that the vast flowering of speculative thought and constructive philosophy which characterized the thirteenth century in western Europe took place in an atmosphere of repression and strict supervision is in serious historical error. Intense, far-ranging discussion and argument, marked by an earnest zeal for truth, was a feature of the milieu in which the schoolmen worked and developed their great synthesis. The *Summa Theologica* and *Summa contra Gentiles* of St. Thomas Aquinas represent the culmination of a long process of intense intellectual activity and free exchange of ideas.[55]

If freedom of expression and teaching is an essential condition for general progress as well as the implementation and pro-

[54] *Liberty and Restraint*, New York, 1931, p. 201.
[55] Any standard work on the subject such as Professor Maurice DeWulf's *History of Medieval Philosophy*, 2 vols., London, 1926, will convey an impression of this process and of the wide scope for difference of views which it involved.

tection of many specific liberties, the mere fact of its existence, however, is unfortunately no guarantee of progress or the preservation of those liberties. We can think of no better case history in the use of liberty to end liberty than the development of the Nazi Party in the Weimar Republic. While the forces which went into the growth of Nazism were exceedingly complex, deriving both from the specific German cultural and political background and the general breakdown of values, economy, and social cohesion in the West, there is no doubt that the liberties which the Nazis enjoyed prior to 1933, foremost among them the liberty to express and propagandize their creed and code of evocative distortions and visceral emotions, were indispensable to the eventual achievement of power.

The sad lessons of history is that truth does not always conquer error in a free competition. In an optimistic liberal era, far-seeing Coventry Patmore could write with realistic cynicism: "Today there is no certainty at all that truth can overcome falsehood in an unrefereed fight, with the latter using brass knuckles, hitting below the belt, and inciting its own interested supporters to riot, the while spectators about the ring become so confused they cannot tell one contestant from the other," [56]—and could ruefully parody the liberal conviction that, despite all vicissitudes, truth and right would win out in the end:

> When all its work is done, the lie shall rot;
> The truth is great, and shall prevail,
> When none cares whether it prevail or not.[57]

The rosy glow which permeated nineteenth century liberal thought derived largely from two doctrines: inevitable progress and the harmony of interests, neither of which has stood up under the onrush of twentieth century events, and a more pro-

[56] Quoted by Ross J. S. Hoffman, *The Will to Freedom*, New York, 1935, p. 88.　　　　[57] Excerpt from poem "Truth."

found study of the human past. But the glow tends to linger on; and even as recently as 1937, Professor Harold Laski could leave unrevised in the latest edition of his *Liberty in the Modern State* such an essentially liberal act of faith as this:

If the view held is untrue, experience shows that conviction of its untruth is invariably a matter of time; it does not come because authority announces it is untrue. If the view is true in part only, the separation of truth and falsehood is accomplished most successfully in a free intellectual competition, a process of dissociation by rational criticism, in which those who hold the false opinion are driven to defend their position on rational grounds.[58]

If Professor Laski's statement corresponded literally to fact, there would be no problem. It obviously does not. Conviction of untruth is not just a matter of time. Men and successions of men have persistently held false and dangerously anti-social views in the past, and will undoubtedly continue to do so until the end of time. Rational criticism of the false is always a good thing; but except for academic discussions, the occasions on which free competition between truth and error remains purely on an intellectual level are rare indeed. The natural tendency of error is to call into its defense all of those irrational factors which can so potently influence the attitudes of men, and sweet reason is soon submerged in a flood of hatreds and prejudices. When the propounders of vicious error finally come into possession of the state's power, "free" competition ceases and access to truth is lost for the populace.

We can agree with Professor Laski that conviction of untruth does not come because authority pronounces it untrue. But that, of course, is not the issue. The purpose of propaganda is

[58] Pelican edition, London, 1937, p. 98. We need hardly add that, in his time, Professor Laski has espoused many causes not all of which are compatible with each other. His present general position can scarcely be called "liberal."

not to convince the propagandist; when it regulates propaganda, authority does so not to change the mind of the propagandist but to prevent him from bringing others to what is conceived to be his harmful point of view.

A similar confusion is found in the argument against the use of force to control expression based on the irrelevancy of force to the claim of truth. It is true that the power of force has no intrinsic relation to truth. Might does not make right, and compulsion can never prove any argument on any subject either true or false. Only realistic examination and analysis in the light of strict logic can do that. But this does not mean that force can have no relation to truth at all. Its legitimate use is not denied in other spheres of activity, although such use always involves a judgment of and distinction between right and wrong, truth and error. Force cannot prove the brutal Nazi concentration camp guard wrong, but those who think he was wrong have prevented him by force from continuing his brutalities. As Felix Adler has pointed out, liberty and force should be contrasted, not reason and force, since force can be an instrument of reason.[59] If freedom of expression and teaching should ordinarily be exempt from the regulation of authority, it must be because the use of force against it endangers certain positive values, not merely because such use against this liberty is *ipso facto* unreasonable.

Just as in the case of freedom of investigation and research, we find upon analysis that there have always been certain desirable limitations to freedom of expression and teaching. It is natural to assume that the expression of lies and errors is more likely to require regulation than the expression of truths, though even the latter may, especially in wartime, be contrary to the general

[59] "The Exercise of Force in the Interest of Freedom," article originally appearing in *The International Journal of Ethics*, April, 1916, reprinted as Appendix II of *An Ethical Philosophy of Life*, New York, 1918.

welfare. While wartime censorships have perpetrated many stupidities, not the least of which is the covering up of blunders and inefficiency, the necessity of such censorship to conceal vital information from the enemy cannot be denied in the light of experience. The whole system of classified information in government, while often abused in peace and war, is based on sound operational necessity. Secret diplomacy and secret treaties as generic terms have been the butt of much criticism, some deserved, but the process of diplomacy and treaty-making must have its secrets along the way if objectives are to be achieved.[60]

When untruth and error are involved, the occasions for desirable regulation of expression are more numerous and commonplace. The law of libel, for example, is based on the sound principle that men do not have a right to tell lies about the conduct or character of other individuals, or even to make defamatory comment on their hidden faults unless such comment serves a public purpose. If its application in Anglo-Saxon countries sometimes seems too harsh, few would want to abolish the entire system of assurance against personal defamation which many centuries of experience have built up. Liberty to cause damage and mental pain to individuals by specific calumny and vicious unnecessary detraction is certainly not one of those liberties which free men feel to be essential.

The development of modern advertising has opened up another whole new field of desirable regulation of expression. Men have always felt it wrong to sell something under false pretenses, to pass off alloy as pure gold. In an economic system where the constant stimulation of new and greater wants is integral to the operation of the productive machine, control of what people say about their products is essential in the public interest; and

[60] For an acute discussion based on long experience of the need for unpublicized negotiation in diplomacy, see Hugh Gibson, *The Road to Foreign Policy*, New York, 1944, Chap. VI.

liberals have been foremost among those advocating more stringent regulation. The effect of such progressive legislation as the various Pure Food and Drug Acts and the Securities Exchange Act has been severely to limit the liberty of manufacturers, distributors, brokers, and investment bankers to express themselves deceptively or inaccurately about the items which they are interested in selling. Those who sponsored these bills had little confidence that truth could here be relied upon to overcome falsehood without the assistance of public authority.

Strictly speaking, no one has a right to propagate falsehood, and in the abstract, every suppression of falsehood promotes the interests of truth. But the state obviously cannot and should not attempt to control every expression of untruth and error. To justify such control, the general welfare must require it and public authority must be competent to decide whether a doctrine at issue is true or false, helpful or harmful. Do these conditions ever apply to the area of the so-called cultural liberties? Needless to say, the debate revolving about this question has been long and acrimonious. The puritan and the libertarian hurl defiance at each other from their extreme positions, as wild and meaningless generalizations obscure the essential issues.

When men speak of the cultural liberties, they usually mean all absences of restraint on those activities which are directed primarily to personal self-expression and self-realization on a non-political and non-economic level. In an era when rigid totalitarianism has attempted to control religious belief and practice, scholarship, literature, and even artistic creation, the tendency among liberals is still to emphasize the complete autonomy of the cultural liberties. Dr. Fosdick has written that "cultural liberties are pursued mainly for their own sake, as ends in themselves, and not as means to some further satisfaction," and that "a man's thoughts, his emotional attachments, his art, literature, religion, and recreation yield him *direct* enjoyment." [61] Even if such a claim were based entirely on fact, this would not mean that cultural activities have no effect on other men and on non-cultural levels. But few if any have ever claimed that the immediate purpose of religious practice is *direct* enjoyment, or even less that religion is something pursued mainly as an end in itself. The age-old debate over whether art can be solely for art's sake has never proved that art may not serve a very utilitarian and non-artistic purpose. Even a man's emotional attachments, directed to the wrong person, may land him in an alienation of affection suit.

A valid defense of the cultural liberties must derive from something more than an ill-conceived autonomy of end. Basically men are cast in the same mold, but they differ greatly in skills, aptitudes, inclinations, and intelligence. Each has a separate personality the perfection of which is attained by the maximum possible development of all good capacities that an individual may possess. Such development largely cannot be forced; it is most real and significant when it is the result of free choice and continued desire for achievement. Government is singularly unfitted to regulate in the cultural sphere, and not only because political administrators often lack the requisite qualifications to make intelligent judgments on the subjects of art, literature, and religion. Because of the wide latitude of opinion existing in this sphere as to true and false, right and wrong, the aim of compulsion is likely to run counter to the judgment and even the moral conviction of a large segment of society, and the interpretation of a broadly drafted regulation must often be based

[61] Dorothy Fosdick, *What Is Liberty?* p. 157. The italicized word is Dr. Fosdick's. It is only fair to mention that her subsequent defense of the cultural liberties is far more sound than the statement with which she begins.

on the enforcing officials' individual prejudices and preferences rather than on any clear-cut, generally accepted criteria of what is desirable in the common good. Abuses of power, petty though some of them may be, become almost inevitable. The history of human endeavor to control expression and teaching is strewn with sad examples of stupidity and misdirected zeal, many of which bear eloquent witness to the usual ineptitude of state action in the sphere of the cultural liberties. Such regulation as is required can generally best be effected through those non-violent pressures which the voluntary associations of men are able to exert.

A sound and realistic policy would therefore allow the broadest possible latitude for the operation of the cultural liberties consistent with common sense and the protection of more desirable liberties. But this implies no complete immunity from regulation by the state under all circumstances. If the state cannot do many things well, there is one thing it can do best, and that is to prevent, by force if necessary, activity which all normally decent men agree to be indubitably wrong and contrary to the general welfare. Few will feel, for example, that any one has the right as a form of self-expression freely to teach children how to be sexual perverts. Only the eccentric would argue that the dope peddler ought to be granted full freedom to advertise his wares as indispensable to the writing of Coleridge-like poetry.

The whole question of obscenity is not one that can be dismissed with a quip about the narrow personal prejudices of Mr. Comstock. We live without doubt in an age of relaxed standards. Many of the restraints of yesterday over the discussion of sex have ceased to exercise their hold upon a franker twentieth century, and this is far from being all to the bad. The puritanic negativism towards sex so characteristic of the Victo-

rian era made a fetish of ignorance and double-talk, and was far
less healthy than the more realistic attitude towards the subject
normally found, for example, in the medieval western world.
But men with decent and sound instincts have always recognized
that there is a great deal of difference between realistic discussion or an earthy joke and the cultivated filth and perversions of
real obscenity, and have consistently felt that purveyors of the
latter should not be permitted unlimited scope to speak and write
for public consumption. One need not be a prude to condemn
pruriency. Those liberals show a rather naive, ivory-tower conception of obscenity who argue that all controls over it are bad
and certain to be abused since, in the past, overzealous censors
have banned a number of books like *Ulysses* and *The Well of
Loneliness* which eminent critics have acclaimed.[62] The standards
of Boston may often seem fickle and absurd, but there are certain standards of minimum decency which public authority
interested in the social health of its citizenry, and particularly
the welfare of its children and adolescents, cannot tolerate.
Obscenity is not essentially theme but method and intent of
treatment. There may be border-line cases, but the genuine
article is not likely to be unrecognizable to persons with a realistic, common sense outlook.

Pre-Hitler Germany provides a fine example of how unrestricted liberty in this sphere can weaken the moral fibre of
a nation and contribute to the growth of movements which
ultimately may deprive the masses of their essential liberties in
other spheres. The situation during the 1920s of obscenity run
riot, described so well by Paul Tabori in his *Epitaph for
Europa*,[63] while partly an effect, was certainly also a contribu-

[62] Professor Laski's argument against such control does not amount to
much more than that. See his *Liberty in the Modern State*, pp. 98–101.
[63] London, 1942, pp. 63 ff.

tory factor to that formlessness, depravity, and moral nihilism which provided such a fertile breeding ground for nazism. The sadism of the Nazis, for example, was not unrelated to the cultivated sadism of Berlin decadents spread throughout the country in numerous pornographic periodicals and "art" publications.

In discussing the political liberties, we shall assume premises which we have stressed earlier in this chapter: that the legitimate authority of the state derives immediately from the consent of the governed and that democracy is the best form of government in the abstract. Without these assumptions, such liberties have little significance or claim to existence. The term political liberty itself is often popularly used in the broad sense of absence of despotic restraint by government within a state. More positively and specifically considered, it may be used as largely synonomous with what we have called *finalistic* liberty, that is, absence of restraint on the sharing of the people in the determination of those particular ends of the state which are meant to achieve the general end of the common good. In an authoritative historical discussion, A. J. Carlyle employs the term in this latter sense.[64] There has been a great European continuity in the theory of political liberty so conceived, broken only by the temporary ascendancy of absolutist theories in the sixteenth and seventeenth centuries. As Professor Carlyle points out, it is a serious misconception to imagine that political liberty,

however important it may have been in Athens and Republican Rome, disappeared in the period of the Roman Empire and in the Middle Ages, and has only been recovered in the last two centuries. . . . In another work my brother and I have endeavoured to write a history of Political Theory in the Middle Ages, and while, in doing

[64] See his *Political Liberty*, Oxford, 1941.

this, we had little if any conscious intention of writing the history of the theory of Political Liberty in those centuries, yet that is what we have actually done.[65]

To generalize further, the individual political liberties are absences of restraint on specific types of activities in the political sphere, and the fundamental political liberties are those which are necessary to the effective functioning of democracy. Whether democratic government can exist in the context of the nation state without the specific representative institutions developed in the Western world during the past several centuries is a moot question. The direct democracy of the ancient Greek city states is, of course, impracticable under the population conditions which prevail today.[66] Historically speaking, as Professor MacIver has pointed out, "the growth of democracy was the growth of parliamentary institutions." [67] It may also be true, as he suggests, that "we must not assume that the free play of public opinion *must* register itself in parliamentary forms. Historical evolution may reveal an endless train of yet undreamed-of modes of government, adaptations to changing needs and changing demands." [68] But the nature of these new modes of government which will permit the free play of public opinion has not yet become clear. In any case, if, as we believe, the essential tests of democracy are the determination of the essential composition of government and of its basic policies by freely manifested public opinion, and the preservation of fundamental liberties on all

[65] *Ibid.*, p. vii. The work to which he refers is, of course, the famous 6-volume *A History of Mediaeval Political Theory in the West*, London and New York, 1903–1936, written by R. W. Carlyle and A. J. Carlyle.
[66] Sir Alfred E. Zimmern's *The Greek Commonwealth*, 3d ed., Oxford, 1922, remains the best general discussion of the Greek *polis*.
[67] R. M. MacIver, *Leviathan and the People*, Baton Rouge, La., 1939, p. 68. He uses the term parliamentary institutions, of course, in the general sense of responsible and representative legislative institutions.
[68] *Ibid.*, p. 69.

levels,[69] it would seem that any mode of government claiming to be democratic must always involve certain specific political liberties. Without freedom for citizens to organize for political purposes, to vote periodically on the issues of who are to have power and of what power shall be permitted to do, to stand for election on terms of equal eligibility, to criticize, to protest, and constantly to keep government within the focus of public opinion, there can be no effective exterior control over the abuse of power on the part of those possessing it at any given time.

In one sense the political liberties are the most essential formal liberties, for they operate on the same level as the physical power of the state. Where they do not exist, uncontrolled state power can attack and jeopardize all the other important liberties of men. *Original* liberty and *finalistic* liberty find their basic expression on this same level through certain formal liberties, while *organizational* liberty itself becomes one of the fundamental political liberties.

Of liberties in the political sphere, freedom of expression and teaching is both the broadest in scope and the first in order of priority. Without freedom of speech, public assembly and publication, the other political liberties would be meaningless; and in actual practice, the end of free expression means the end of all fundamental political liberties. The Nazi plebiscites were, of course, a mockery of the electoral process. Any justifiable control of freedom of expression and teaching on the political level implies, therefore, justifiable control of other political activities involving the same object of regulation.

As we write this in the close post-war period, the daily press

[69] Professor MacIver describes the second of these tests in terms of recognition of the distinction between state and community, a distinction necessary in the proper designation of state function and hence of the area of desirable liberty. *Ibid.*, pp. 70–76.

already makes frequent reference to the attempts of fascist groups in the United States and England, some with little more than changed labels, to consolidate their forces and regain strength. Should their attempts at meeting and propaganda be suppressed in democratic states now when they present no immediate threat to its institutions and liberties? Writers of indignant "letters to the editor" say yes, by all means, at once and completely. Others will agree with the attitude, as reported in the press, of the British Home Secretary, Mr. Chuter Ede, who in referring to an attempt of the Britons' Action League, a Mosleyite offshoot, to organize a meeting in London, expressed the opinion that this kind of affair required no government action but could best be left to the humor of the British people. Only prophetic powers, which are generally not given to the rulers of men, can guarantee that the test of events will prove a policy sound and truly wise. If the Weimar politicos could have foreseen the events of the next two decades, they would probably have shown less leniency towards the incipient Nazi movement.

Policy in such cases must be based on an assessment of probabilities, on a calculation of risk. A political doctrine subversive in theory may never become dangerously subversive in fact; and the atmosphere of healthy democracy can stand a great deal of theoretical subversiveness without becoming contaminated. Much depends also on the absorptive capacity of a specific country. A small democracy like Switzerland can obviously not tolerate that volume of anti-democratic teaching and propaganda which a giant like the United States may well shrug off, and few will claim that during the war Switzerland lost any of the essential quality of her democracy because, though not a belligerent, she outlawed the Nazi and Communist parties and denied the free expression of their ideas. If it seems to a democratic government that the continued teaching and propagation of anti-democratic ideals by an organized group threatens to create a situation in which that group can become sufficiently strong to seize power, then its right to act seems clear. Not to act is to sacrifice the welfare of society for a quixotic ideal of absolute freedom, to give untruth and viciousness full scope to use all of their distortions, slanders, and unfair tactics against truth and decency, which are prevented by their very nature from using the same methods of appealing to men's lower instincts. If the proper function of the state is to secure and defend those external conditions necessary to the fullest achievement of personality, it certainly cannot be denied the right to intervene against the danger of conditions which negate that ideal.

Such a realistic attitude is far removed from the naive nineteenth century assumption that truth would always win out in a free slugging match with error! The price of liberty is indeed eternal vigilance, not only of citizens against the state, but of the democratic state against those who would capture power to end liberty. But this does not require a perpetual witch hunt. The United States can tolerate a great luxuriance of political exoticisms without clear and substantial danger. To attempt suppression of every subversive doctrine and group would involve far worse evils than to permit broad and continuing freedom of expression and teaching. As we have emphasized, violent compulsion is never a good thing in itself; at best, it is the lesser of two evils one or the other of which is necessary. Where there is no reasonable certitude that state repressive action will serve the general welfare in a manner proportionate to the evil involved in such action, there can be no justification for the control of political expression and teaching. Where there is doubt, the burden of proof is always on the side of violence.

Such a position is not inconsistent with an enlightened liberal political outlook, if that outlook is not linked to an unrealistic concept of inevitable progress. As Professor Hoffman has pointed out, a liberal like Mill assumed that society had advanced to a stage far beyond that barbarism to which it could never return but which, he was quite willing to admit, had required despotic rule.[70] The twentieth century has brought new barbarisms and new despotisms the answer to which is not more despotism but strong, purposeful democracy unafraid to take those measures, in time and without wavering, which the protection of its basic values requires. The important thing is that physical compulsion be recognized for what it is—at best, a necessary means, a *sine qua non* to a good end, but never a desirable way of achieving objectives that can otherwise be attained; at worst, a form of power which is the main strength of tyranny and oppression; and always a dangerous weapon, easily liable to abuse and, if much abused, capable of undermining the entire structure of a democratic state and the mortar of general will which holds it together.

To endure today, democracy cannot fight merely a defensive battle. To preserve the political liberties is not enough if liberties on other levels of activity are lacking which it is likewise a proper state function to secure. Perhaps the chief test of democracy's capacity to survive in our time is its ability to cope with the problems of liberty in the economic sphere. The conflict of specific economic liberties is more frequent, and the exercise of some liberties more preclusive of other liberties, than in the cultural or even the political sphere; and such broad, generally approved legislation as the Pure Food and Drug Acts and the Securities Exchange Act imposes far more stringent con-

[70] Ross J. S. Hoffman, *The Will to Freedom*, New York, 1935, p. 99.

trols on freedom of expression and action than could ever properly be attempted in the other spheres.

It seems quite clear that complete liberty of economic activity is incompatible with that maximum development of each individual personality which is the end of liberty in society. The economically depressed portion of a country's population, living in squalid slums and faced with a daily struggle for bare necessities, can scarcely hope for those good things of life without which most men cannot attain their fullest growth. Talented and fortunate individuals may rise out of their milieu, but for the majority of the poor, the term economic liberty has a hollow ring indeed. Unless the state fosters and maintains primary economic justice for all its citizens, it is derelict in its duty.

Some have attempted to call a halt to the development of the modern social service state by arguing that increasing government power over individual economic activity must inevitably end in economic serfdom, in a deprivation not only of every economic liberty but of the other fundamental liberties as well.[71] Coming from advocates of an outmoded economic liberalism, such warnings are likely to make little impression upon the masses who aspire to social justice. The cry that state encroachment will end basic economic liberties can hardly appeal to those who have never enjoyed them, just as the old liberal criterion of Herbert Spencer which would permit each man to enjoy "freedom to do all that he wills, provided he infringes not the equal freedom of any other man,"[72] actually has little relevance to a complex industrial society, where the means of

---

[71] Professor Friedrich A. Hayek's much-publicized *The Road to Serfdom*, Chicago, 1945, is perhaps the best-known work espousing this thesis.
[72] *Social Statics*, New York, 1896, p. 55.

enjoying equal economic liberty are completely lacking to many, and the liberties of some can deprive others of *different* liberties which they likewise prize highly.

There is certainly a danger to the fundamental liberties in the growth of state power over economic life, a danger perhaps most clearly grasped by members of the modern agrarian-distributist movement. More than thirty years ago, Hilaire Belloc in his *The Servile State* [73] gave classical expression to the distributist interpretation of the anti-libertarian tendencies of our industrial society with its uprooted proletarian masses and formless agglomorations of population; and events have yet to prove his analysis wrong in essentials. Certainly the health of society demands more than a frequent shot in the arm with social legislation, and the conditions of maximum freedom involve a fine balance between individual, society, and state which an industrial civilization—at least as we know it—can scarcely attain. Any long-range program of legislation directed to the ultimate broadening of liberties must accordingly do more than merely prevent the specific abuse of liberty by some; it must also aim to create the most favorable economic environment for the enjoyment of the fundamental liberties.

THE LIBERTY OF THE STATE

Apart from the problem of individual liberty within the state, there is also the problem of liberty between states—a problem largely of excess of liberty rather than its deficiency. Weaker states may, of course, and all too often do, lose their liberty to stronger states which ride roughshod over them in conquest. By ending national liberties in a most cruel and absolute manner,

[73] London, 1912. See also Belloc's *The Restoration of Property*, London and New York, 1936, for a more recent statement of his distributist philosophy.

our modern tyrannies have brought new stress to the values involved in the old Greek concept of liberty as liberty of the city state as a whole against foreign domination. But even in the case of conquest, the problem may be stated as one of too much liberty for the conquering state combined with a lack of necessary regulatory power in the international society. The liberty of a state to use aggressive force against another state in the achievement of selfish *national* objectives does not serve a truly functional purpose and is therefore always ethically unjustified. The moral law applies to state action just as much as to individual action, and in an ideal world, all the rulers of men would recognize that fact and formulate policy in the light of principles other than those of pure national selfishness and aggrandizement. While the state's primary function is to seek the general welfare of its citizens, it cannot properly do so by ignoring the welfare of other states and other peoples, just as the well-ordered individual life cannot be based merely on selfish personal desires and needs but must involve consideration and service for others. The principle of competition is a healthy one both within and between states, provided it operates inside a framework of shared basic purposes and mutual regard for the general welfare. Without the striving to do better, to build finer, to achieve more, stagnation is inevitable; but such striving must be conditioned by a strong regard for ethical principles which ban the unfair act, the deliberate distortion, the misused power.

The international realities of today are evidently far from an ideal equilibrium of competition and cooperation. The liberty of states is still inadequately subject to restraints similar to those imposed by legal systems which operate within civilized states to afford protection to individual rights against the abuse of liberty, although the United Nations organization is an attempted beginning on the political level of the process of bringing external manifestations of state power within the orbit of collective rather than selfish purpose. No man of good will can do other than wish it well. On the political level alone can concerted action, based on firm principles of moral law, create the necessary conditions for viable positive law. A comprehensive system of international law will develop only when the association of states in the greater society has become strong enough to prevent individual states from deviating from the common purpose of maintaining peace, security, and justice. As Professor J. L. Brierly has put it,

Law never creates order; the most it can do is to help to sustain order when that has once been firmly established, for it sometimes acquires a prestige of its own which enables it to foster an atmosphere favorable to the continuance of orderly social relations when these are called upon to stand a strain. But always there has to be order before law can even begin to take root and grow. When the circumstances are propitious, law is the sequel, but it is never the instrument, of the establishment of order.[74]

Some argue like Emery Reves that peace cannot come until a universal legal order in a world state replaces the present anarchical relationship of national sovereignties.[75] It may well be that the instabilities of state power can never satisfactorily be controlled otherwise, but that should not prevent effort for peace in the light of present possibilities. Sound ethical theory has never had place for the concept of absolute sovereignty, yet even the atomic bomb threat cannot radically modify in a day the faulty political philosophies and institutional developments of several centuries.

Others maintain with Professor E. H. Carr that "the world will have to accommodate itself to the emergence of a few great

[74] *The Outlook for International Law*, Oxford, 1944, p. 74.
[75] See his *The Anatomy of Peace*, New York, 1945.

multi-national units in which power will be mainly concentrated," and which will represent a compromise between anarchic liberty and world authority.[76] Within these large units, the ideal relationship of large component to small component will be based on the principle of the "good neighbor." Such an arrangement, it is claimed, is provided for by the special role assigned to the great powers in the United Nations organization.

But whatever the degree of liberty which the actual trend of events leaves to individual states, the ethical principles involved are clear and point the way in which the ideal international organization should develop. The international community is definitely a functional reality, although the implications of that fact continue largely to be unrealized. In the seventeenth century, the great Spanish philosopher, Francisco Suárez, could write that

the human race, howsoever many the various peoples and kingdoms into which it may be divided, always preserves a certain unity not only as a species, but also, as it were, a moral and political unity called for by the natural precept of mutual love and mercy, which applies to all, even to strangers of any nation.

Therefore, although a given sovereign state, commonwealth, or kingdom, may constitute a perfect community in itself, consisting of its own members, nevertheless, each one of these states is also, in a certain sense, and viewed in relation to the human race, a member of that universal society; for never are these states, when standing alone, so self-sufficient that they do not require some mutual assistance, association and intercourse, at times for their greater welfare and advantage, but at other times because also of some moral necessity or lack, as is clear from experience.[77]

[76] *Nationalism and After*, London, 1945, p. 52.
[77] Francisco Suárez, *Tractatus de Legibus ac Deo Legislatore*, trans. of selection in James Brown Scott, *The Spanish Conception of International Law and of Sanctions*, Washington, 1934, p. 90.

Unfortunately, the existence of an international community does not in itself guarantee the development of authoritative organs which can effectively carry out its purpose. There is no reply on an ethical level to the argument of Francisco de Vitoria that "the world as a whole, being in a way one single State, has the power to create laws that are just and fitting for all persons, as are the rules of international law"; [78] but, as we have seen, political order must precede legal order. Any organization, therefore, which brings the real closer to the rational is good and worthy of support.

In the ideal international order, individual states would be entitled to no more liberty than the fulfillment of their function demands. In certain spheres, this would entail a great measure of liberty, but it would likewise mean the end of liberty to use force as an instrument of national policy. Only cooperative use of force would be legitimate, if necessary to impose international control over a recalcitrant state that has breached the peace. Although such a delimitation of state liberty is obviously not compatible with absolutist theories of sovereignty, it need not, in the long run, actually involve a net loss of liberties. Just as in the case of individuals, less freedom for some to do certain things may mean greater liberty for many to do other things, so the end of state liberty to use violent power against other states might well bring additional liberties to all states, both with reference to one another and in the formulation of internal policy. The cessation of fear and the advent of real security would undoubtedly release new energies for constructive purposes, and permit the development of many new modes of desirable activity unhampered by the exigencies of national defense.

[78] Francisco de Vitoria, *De Potestate Civili*, written 1528, trans. in James Brown Scott, *The Spanish Origin of International Law*, Part I, *Francisco de Vitoria and his Law of Nations*, Oxford, 1934, Appendix C, p. lxxi.

In this transition period between two worlds, for better or for worse, men of good will can strive for the growth and success of that international authority and its concomitant institutions which are now still largely in the pristine state. But states will reserve the right, no matter how regretfully, to anticipate and in a measure prepare for the possible failure of these attempts at general order and security—a failure the implications of which men can well dread. In such a turn of events, the ethical principles of the just war, which we have discussed in a previous chapter, will have pertinence, though the Lord alone knows what role ethical considerations can play in the battle of the atoms which is foretold.

SUMMING UP

This has been a long chapter, but the relationship of authority and liberty which it discusses is basic to the problem of power and its expression in concrete human activity. When a satisfactory relationship between the two is attained in every sphere of activity, then for that time and place the problem of power is solved. Such perfect solutions unfortunately are not for this world, which will always contain imperfection, falsehood, and selfish ambition. The best mankind can hope for is a general tendency, in a given period, towards the control of power by morals, and by legitimate national and international authority sanctioned by morals—a tendency which the inevitable abuses of power cannot essentially frustrate. Every justifiable liberty is a natural right which authority has the duty to respect, and if the general welfare so demands, to protect by positive action.

The majority of us tend to be complacent about liberty, to take it too much for granted until it is threatened. We appreciate it most when we are in danger of losing it. Liberty is a favorite subject of poets, but largely in terms of crisis. If individual liberty is not an end in itself, it is certainly a most necessary means to the fulfillment of personality. Its value rises out of the free wills of men to whom such liberty is given as part of a great mystery of purpose, with the final end not predestined but to be chosen. The human conscience cannot be forced, nor can the free choice of individuals, to do that which is contrary to good conscience. Hence any attempt by the state to ban immoral personal conduct, simply because it is immoral, would go beyond the proper function of force. In Christian theology, "God so prized man's free service that He preferred a humanity sinful but free to a humanity of compulsory righteousness." [79] But when the liberty of some adversely affects the liberties of others to a point where the lesser evil is to curb the former, then authority can legitimately intervene.

Liberty may be good or bad, it "may be sacred or it may be despicable. Liberty is the final condition of all progress, but the very same name is inscribed on the banners of the blindest and most selfish defenders of unjust privilege old or new." [80] The exercise of every liberty that one chooses is not necessarily synonomous with the enjoyment of maximum liberty. The chronic alcoholic has lost his freedom in the very process of doing that which he has been free to do. Nor does mere defiance of established moral codes, as so many "emancipated moderns" believe, alone constitute "real" liberty. It is quite possible, in fact, that liberty to indulge in licentious personal conduct may exist side by side with rigid tyranny in other spheres, as in the decadent period of ancient Rome. Henry Nevinson has written that, although political and civil liberty were practically nonexistent in Tsarist Russia, he found there greater freedom of thought and freedom from social convention than in England.[81]

[79] E. I. Watkin, *A Philosophy of Form*, New York, 1935, p. 178.
[80] R. M. MacIver, *Community*, London, 3d ed., 1924, p. 317.
[81] *England's Voice of Freedom*, London, 1929, p. 13.

The fundamental liberties, as discussed in this chapter, are those which the collective experience of mankind has shown to be most essential to the perfection of human nature and hence primary requisites of maximum liberty. If, from one point of view, a legitimate role of state authority is to maximize liberty by controlling certain liberties which work against the greatest enjoyment of liberty by the many, then such role in the concrete amounts essentially to the assertion and protection of the fundamental liberties. This is far from espousing that negative concept of the "policeman state" which, to a large extent, vitiated nineteenth century liberal thinking. For we have come to a better understanding of both the basic incompatibility of some liberties with others that are more important and the need for positive state action, in many instances, to create or to foster conditions necessary for the exercise of certain fundamental liberties as well as to achieve those other objectives desirable in the general welfare which individuals or social units smaller than the state cannot achieve. The extent of permissible state action is determined not by arbitrary delimitation but by the requirements of the common good.

Conclusion

As FAR AS the ultimate control of power is concerned, the important thing today, as always, is that the possessors of power regard it as a trust to be exercised in the general welfare rather than simply a means to selfish ends, whether personal or national. The rulers of men must be men of good will, and they must have strong and valid principles as guide to their general purpose. But both experience and common sense indicate that, especially in an era of cultural disintegration and moral chaos like the present, such good will and principles must be grounded on a sound general philosophy if they are not to be swept away by the prevailing turmoil and ever-present temptation to abuse of power. The corrupting tendency of power is free to do its worst where there are no decisive ethical inhibitions as to its use, even among those who may start out with altruistic if vague intentions; and men of perverted will and dominant personality, ruthlessly logical in carrying out the implications of their amoral philosophies, eventually come to complete power when good will lacks the support of strong moral conviction.

In the preceding chapters we have attempted to outline a system of concepts and principles which can provide that ethical basis for politics so greatly needed in our time. The theory propounded is not linked by necessity to any specific culture or physical environment; it claims to derive from certain basic facts of man's nature and his role in the universe which are independent of time, place, and circumstance. It admittedly implies a belief in the rationality of the universe which may well seem unacceptable to many moderns. Criticism on this score is possible. But the issue must then be stated clearly. There is no halfway stop. The universe is either rational and purposive, or it is not. If it is not, then Bertrand Russell's dismal epitaph on human hope is the only realism: "Brief and powerless is man's life, on him and all his race the slow sure doom falls pitiless and dark. Blind to good and evil, reckless of destruction, omnipotent matter rolls on its relentless way."[1] If men are nothing but fortuitous collocations of atoms in the macrocosm, mere specks of animated dust, soon to be snuffed out, on a small rock floating through illimitable space, then true logic rests only with those who, having scorned the law of nature for the philosophy it involves, refuse to grasp feebly for palliatives but boldly become advocates of ruthless *Machtpolitik*, of Machiavellianism, of the rule of sheer expediency and egoism, of complete disregard for all rights and duties if one can get away with it. If the universe is irrational, then the irrational law of tooth and fang, of instinct and force, is highest morality.

Most men, of course, are reluctant to be so cruelly logical when such logic goes against their better instincts and against the ethical heritage of many centuries. Even the eloquent despair of a modern Lucretius like Lord Russell leads him not to the espousal of suicide but to a defiant if ill-founded assertion of personality in the face of an inexorable and impersonal universe. In his recent work *A History of Western Philosophy*,[2] he comes no closer to resolving the basic contradiction in his approach. He sides with Buddha as against Nietzsche, but does "not know how to prove that he is right by any argument such as can be used in a mathematical or scientific question." He opposes Nietzsche "because he [Nietzsche] likes the contemplation of pain, because he erects conceit into a duty, because the

[1] *Mysticism and Logic*, New York, 1925, p. 56.
[2] New York, 1945.

men whom he most admires are conquerors, whose glory is cleverness in causing men to die." But he can offer nothing more in rebuttal than to claim that "the ultimate argument against his philosophy, as against any unpleasant but internally self-consistent ethic, lies not in an appeal to facts, but in an appeal to the emotions." [3] That obviously is no argument at all for those whose emotions tend otherwise, or who are torn by powerful conflicting emotions, by the lust for power and the restraints of charity and justice. It is no real argument even for those who favor Russell's point of view emotionally, but find their selfish interests opposed.

In any case the Bertrand Russells of our time, who have contributed their bit to undermining what is left of the traditional codes, are being swept aside by ruthless men of less sensibility but more logic. Many humanitarian liberals have been living purely off the heritage of the ethical past. Espousing traditional Western political and social ideals, they have proceeded to deny away every reason for accepting them by rejecting the philosophy from which they derive. Such an unreal structure of moral imperatives is doomed to collapse; for it is impossible to preserve the positive values in a political or social theory while repudiating their metaphysical and epistemological basis, just as it is a "fundamental illusion" to believe "that it is possible to conserve all of positive and constructive value in the Christian order while removing from it the belief in God." [4]

A point of utmost importance which cannot be stressed often enough is the complete rationality of totalitarian methods, even the atrocities, once the initial premises are granted. And those premises, as we have attempted to show, are linked inextricably with the historic denial of the philosophic basis for the tradi-

[3] *A History of Western Philosophy*, p. 772.
[4] Rosalind Murray, *The Good Pagan's Failure*, London, 1939, p. 135.

tional moral values. There are two facts in this twentieth century world which any realistic person must face: the horrible capacity of man for cruelty and terror once the control of morals is removed, and the potentiality for destruction which modern instruments of force place in the hands of those who possess power. The introduction of theological considerations is not necessary to prove to our era that there is a latent capacity for evil in man which the nineteenth century had forgotten and which, when it comes to the surface, must confound those unrealistic optimists who have felt that the road of mankind is inevitably upwards towards a more generalized kindness, sweetness, and light. This capacity for evil is no abstraction, no vagary, no imaginative hangover of Calvinism, but an observable phenomenon which social scientists as well as moralists must take into consideration. A study of the conditions under which it finds fullest expression can lead, we believe, to no other conclusion than that the restoration of a moral basis for personal and political conduct is the only hope for that maximization of justice, order, and liberty which all men of good will desire.

The claim has been made that the real threat today is not "unprincipled men" but men fanatically devoted to the principles of revolutionary morality, men with a terrific inner certainty about truth. Such a statement of the problem suffers from the basic defect of failing to distinguish between the slogans and enthusiasms which are used to stimulate the masses and the actual motivations of those who lead. A study of the Nazi aims and methods, supplemented by information now possible to obtain in post-war Germany, will, we believe, convince that the element of ethical idealism, even in a very perverted sense, was largely lacking among the Nazi leaders. There was, it is true, especially in the balmy days of seemingly unending victory, a certain intoxication of success, and even to the end some members of his personal entourage continued to display an irrational devotion to the Fuehrer. But this was something quite different from that devotion to principle which is implied as characteristic of the Nazi leadership among others. The typical amoral leader of our time, be he Nazi, Fascist, or Communist, "uses" the revolutionary morality to justify the complete repudiation of traditional morality as a means to his ultimate end of power. His approach is essentially cold-blooded and entirely opportunistic in the choice of means to achieve a selfish objective, which itself can be justified only in terms of a relativistic philosophy under which the achievement of power and all it brings becomes the *ultimo ratio*. To classify the totalitarian leaders of our time as ethical idealists is to misapprehend the nature of the forces at work in this twentieth century and of the intellectual history that lies back of the contemporary amoral quest for power. We are now reaping the harvest of an ideological process by which the bases for ethical idealism were destroyed, with the dominant philosophies of the day, in their implications, providing a complete rationale of amoralism.

Properly understood, the basic premises of the traditional morality can be rationally acceptable to the modern man of intelligence who is abreast of developments in science and philosophy. We believe that a revival of conviction as to the validity of human knowledge, the fact of man's free will, and the unique value of the individual person—and all that this implies in the way of basic philosophy—is not automatically precluded by the advance of knowledge in the twentieth century but, if anything, is favored thereby. Certainly the crudities of early Freudianism and behaviorism, with their relativism and ironclad determinism, have long been discarded; and modern physical and biological research has uncovered nothing incompatible with a finalistic interpretation of reality. Mechanistic materialism is no longer such a prevailing fashion in the laboratories and observatories. In books published only short periods apart three eminent scientists, Sir Edmund Whittaker, F. Sherwood Taylor, and Lecomte du Noüy, have recently testified to the teleological implications of new theories in physics and biology.[5] While philosophy can stand on its own feet within its order of knowledge and need not change major premises with every fluctuation in scientific theory,[6] it obviously must incorporate truth from all sources into its conclusions; and any tendency among scientists towards the assertion of personality and purpose is at least a favorable omen in this science-minded age for the restoration of belief in those premises which are the necessary basis for sound ethics.

In writing of the necessary epistemological basis for morals, we have attempted to show that without the prior assumption that, under given circumstances, man can attain certain knowledge of objective truth, no ethical system can have validity.[7] This is not to equate scientific truth with moral truth. But the latter does involve a form of certitude which cannot be watered down to mere probability. Though it cannot be proved in a test tube, moral truth possesses validity within its own order of knowledge. We can be certain that an action is wrong in terms of our criteria, and we can be certain that these criteria derive logically from a consistent philosophy of values which itself rests on a firm basis demanding rational assent. To deny the possibility of moral certitude in either of these two senses is to deny any pos-

---

[5] See Sir Edmund Whittaker, *Space and Spirit*, London, 1946; F. Sherwood Taylor, *Two Ways of Life*, London, 1947; Lecomte du Noüy, *Human Destiny*, New York, 1947.
[6] See Jacques Maritain, *The Degrees of Knowledge*, trans. Bernard Wall, New York, 1938, for a brilliant discussion of the relationship between science and philosophy. [7] See above, pp. 59 ff.

sible validity to ethics. No better exemplification of this truth need be sought than the process in intellectual history by which, in our time, men have lost their ethical convictions, ending in the production of such highly intelligent, primarily selfish, and completely amoral graspers for power as Goebbels, Goering, and Bormann.

We have endeavored in Chapters VI and VII to apply the natural law approach (discussed in Chapter V) to the two great general problems of power: the use of violence and the relation between authority and liberty. One need have little hesitancy in saying that the principles outlined will be acceptable to the man of good will and, allowing perhaps for minor variations on particular points, would be those which he would advance after giving thought to the specific problems in each situation. The claim is legitimate that this is but another instance of the universal content of the natural law ethic. To those who would still question the necessity of such a theoretical foundation for agreed-upon principles, we can only repeat again that the validity of an ethical system depends not only on its appeal to sentiment, or on its ability to draw on the emotional reservoir left by the traditional morality, but on its complete logical derivation from a coherent philosophy of values. Only a moral code which has consistent rational appeal can hope to recapture the mind and fire the imagination of twentieth century man.

No claim is made, however, that modern man will actually return to that general acceptance of morality which alone makes possible the maximum control of power in accordance with non-selfish standards of justice and charity. There is a great reserve of good will in the world; the tragedy lies in its loss of focal point. We may hope that the basic common sense of the race will again, as on occasions in the past, break through current mists and obscurities to discard those distortions and misinterpretations which have sent individuals and nations off on a moral tangent. But guarantee there is none. The pessimists may well be right. Our era may mark the retrogressive stage of a culture cycle as part of a vast historical process which will work itself out before a young and healthier culture again comes to the fore, embodying sound moral values that claim general allegiance. While Oswald Spengler's seasonal concept of the cyclical movement of history is undoubtedly too rigid, the culture cycle theories of such historians and sociologists as Christopher Dawson, P. A. Sorokin, and Arnold Toynbee have given us a new frame of reference for the understanding of history.[8] There is no such thing as inevitable progress. Whole cultures may sink into ruin and oblivion; others may congeal into sterility. The culture of the West may likewise lose its vitality, fall prey to divisive and destructive forces, and finally collapse. As a matter of fact, under the impact of the atomic bomb and other new techniques of warfare, the classic culture cycle may no longer be allowed to work itself out. The newly unleashed powers of physical violence can wipe out a culture at its height, or at any stage. Those who have seen the ubiquitous and dismal ruins of Germany since the end of the last pre-atomic war in Europe need no further warning of the fact that, unless the power that men now have can be controlled, the institutions and mode of life we cherish are certainly doomed to destruction. The rubble of once-mighty cities, which it took many centuries to build but only a relatively few days to destroy, bears overwhelming witness to the need for continuing

[8] See Christopher Dawson, *Progress and Religion*, London, 1929; P. A. Sorokin, *Social and Cultural Dynamics*, 4 vols., New York, 1937–1941; Arnold J. Toynbee, *A Study of History*, 6 vols., London, 1934–1939.

peace in this twentieth century world. The next time preponderant power may be on the side of tyranny rather than with the traditional values struggling to survive.

If progress is far from inevitable, so too is retrogression. Men can meet the challenge of this critical period and change the course of history. A return to the sources of its moral strength can save our culture and begin a new upward cycle of development. The ethical inhibition of power-abuse may obtain to a point where aggressive war ceases to be an instrument of policy. At best such a world will still be far from Utopia. Misuse of the liberty which power gives will always be with us. There will always be those like the Don Giovanni of Mozart's opera who shout "Long live liberty," as they crush two peasant girls to themselves. And perhaps there will always be would-be Hitlers to attempt the seizure of power. If the moral structure of society is sound, however, they will not succeed in misleading the masses and perverting the activities of entire nations.

Abuse of power is something men must always fear, but power rightly used is the basis of civilization. Power without morals is the scourge of mankind. Power with morals is mankind's greatest servant. Before the trend towards amoralism in the use of power can be halted, a great task of clarification and reeducation must be accomplished. Let us hope that men will come to appreciate this urgent necessity and succeed in restoring a viable basis for that ethical control of power which alone, especially now that the tools of power have become so destructive, is the condition of mankind's progress and, indeed, continued existence.

Index